EMERSON AND THE HISTORY OF RHETORIC

EMERSON *and the* HISTORY OF RHETORIC

Roger Thompson

Southern Illinois University Press | *Carbondale*

Southern Illinois University Press
www.siupress.com

20 19 18 17 4 3 2 1

Cover and title page illustration: cropped portrait of Ralph Waldo Emerson. Ralph Waldo Emerson Collection, Yale Collection of American Literature, Beinecke Rare Book and Manuscript Library (YCA MSS 212; 5 × 4 in. daguerreotype)

Library of Congress Cataloging-in-Publication Data
Names: Thompson, Roger (Roger Charles), author.
Title: Emerson and the history of rhetoric / Roger Thompson.
Description: Carbondale : Southern Illinois University Press, 2017. | Includes bibliographical references and index.
Identifiers: LCCN 2017008904 | ISBN 9780809336128 (paperback) | ISBN 9780809336135 (e-book)
Subjects: LCSH: Emerson, Ralph Waldo, 1803–1882—Criticism and interpretation. | Narration (Rhetoric)—History. | Discourse analysis, Literary. | BISAC: LANGUAGE ARTS & DISCIPLINES / Rhetoric. | LITERARY CRITICISM / American / General. | LANGUAGE ARTS & DISCIPLINES / Speech.
Classification: LCC PS1638 .T53 2017 | DDC 814/.3—dc23
LC record available at https://lccn.loc.gov/2017008904

Printed on recycled paper. ♲

For my parents, who taught me the value of nature, expression, and self-reliance

CONTENTS

ACKNOWLEDGMENTS

My sincere thanks to the reviewers who helped shape this book. They provided invaluable guidance and support in its development. My thanks to Shaun Allshouse, the cover designer of this volume, and the Southern Illinois University Press staff, especially Karl Kageff, Kristine Priddy, Linda Buhman, Amy Alsip, and the editorial staff, for their enthusiasm for this project and their incomparable work ethic. My thanks to *College English* and *Philosophy and Rhetoric* for permission to reprint some of this work. Parts of chapter 1 are taken from "Emerson and the Democratization of Plato's 'True Rhetoric,'" *Philosophy and Rhetoric* 48.2 (2015): 117–38. Sections of chapter 4 previously appeared as "'Habit of Heat': Emerson, Belletristic Rhetoric, and the Role of the Imagination," *College English* 69.3 (Jan. 2007): 260–82, copyright © 2007 by the National Council of Teachers of English. Quotations from Emerson's "New England" lecture and sermons found in chapters 1 and 4 are from the Ralph Waldo Emerson Memorial Association deposit, Houghton Library, Harvard University.

Several people deserve special mention. First, Fred Erisman, for his mentorship and passion for Emerson, and Rich Enos, for fooling me into believing that manuscript research might break down disciplinary boundaries. Phyllis Cole's endless intellectual curiosity remains one of my great inspirations, and it has shaped the Ralph Waldo Emerson Society and fostered new avenues of inquiry for all of us. Steven Mailloux unwittingly taught me that disciplinary boundaries are fluid, and the American Society for the History of Rhetoric graciously endured some of my early investigations into Emerson's rhetoric. Without Linda Walker and J. R. LeMaster, I would have never discovered Emerson, and Linda's dedication to her students serves as a model for me to this day. I thank the Houghton Library and the Virginia Military Institute faculty development committee for funding my research; the expertise of the Houghton librarians is humbling. Without Lois Agnew, Amy Heckathorn, Julie Smith, and Joonna Trapp, and without my recalcitrant, insubordinate, and incorrigible colleagues from the Virginia Military Institute, I simply would not have completed this project. Thank you all for years of support, dedication, and encouragement. Finally, I thank my wife—for giving me time, tolerance, motivation, and love throughout the long years of this book coming to life.

WORKS FREQUENTLY CITED

This study follows the standardized abbreviations established by Emerson scholars for his work. Whenever possible, I have used the most authoritative text available, which is most frequently to be found either in Emerson's *Collected Works*, whose final volume was issued to great anticipation in 2013, or in his *Journals and Miscellaneous Notebooks*. When referencing manuscripts, I have followed the practice of citing the library record at Harvard University's Houghton Library.

CW	*The Collected Works of Ralph Waldo Emerson*. Ed. Robert E. Spiller et al. 10 vols. Cambridge, MA: Harvard University Press, 1971–2013.
EL	*The Early Lectures of Ralph Waldo Emerson*. Ed. Stephen E. Whicher, Robert E. Spiller, and Wallace E. Williams. 3 vols. Cambridge, MA: Harvard University Press, 1959–72.
JMN	*The Journals and Miscellaneous Notebooks of Ralph Waldo Emerson*. Ed. William H. Gilman et al. 16 vols. Cambridge, MA: Harvard University Press, 1960–82.
Letters	*The Letters of Ralph Waldo Emerson*. Ed. Ralph L. Rusk and Eleanor M. Tilton. 10 vols. New York: Columbia University Press, 1939.
LL	*The Later Lectures of Ralph Waldo Emerson, 1843–1871*. Ed. Ronald A. Bosco and Joel Myerson. 2 vols. Athens: University of Georgia Press, 2001.

TN	*The Topical Notebooks of Ralph Waldo Emerson.* Ed. Ralph H. Orth et al. 3 vols. Columbia: University of Missouri Press, 1990–94.
W	*The Complete Works of Ralph Waldo Emerson.* With a biographical introduction and notes by Edward Waldo Emerson. Centenary ed. 12 vols. Boston: Houghton Mifflin, 1903–4.

EMERSON AND THE HISTORY OF RHETORIC

INTRODUCTION
The Architect of Discourse

In a journal entry that has largely escaped notice, Ralph Waldo Emerson insists that "all conversation & all literature is rhetoric" (*TN* 2: 144). This declaration comes in a journal he kept on the topic of rhetoric, *Notebook RT*, which he began in 1857 or 1858. Written on the third page of the notebook—the previous two have barely one hundred words between them—the idea must have been an early addition to his thinking on rhetoric. The precise context for the idea is difficult to determine, as context is hard to pin down for virtually all his notebooks because they function as a kind of clearing house of thoughts, quotations, and records, but he cross-references the entry to another one made in a different journal. More interestingly, just a few pages later (*TN* 2: 145), he expands on the quotation. Invoking one of the giants in rhetorical history, he writes, "All conversation, as all literature, appears to me the pleasure of rhetoric, or, I may say, of metonymy. 'To make the great, little, & the little, great to make motes mountains, & mountains motes—' Isocrates said, 'was the orator's office.' Well, that is what poetry & thinking do" (*TN* 2: 145). Emerson gathers oratory, conversation, literature, poetry, and thinking here under the topic of rhetoric, and in doing so, he joins fields of study separated within today's academy while prefiguring the heart of contemporary rhetorical theory: the necessary relationship between cognition and expression.

Emerson's relevance to literary studies has never really been questioned. While some might dislike his style or quibble about the degree or direction of his influence, few dismiss his impact. By contrast, Emerson has yet to receive full treatment as a rhetorician, a rhetorical theorist, or a philosopher of rhetoric, despite widespread agreement that he was important to the American rhetorical scene, both as a career orator and an incisive commentator on the rise of the podium in the nineteenth century. Emerson's importance, however, extends well beyond simply commentator or speaker. He, in fact, theorizes the role of rhetoric in a society—as it emerged in both oral and written forms. He discusses the topics of rhetoric, oratory, and eloquence frequently, even in his poetry and in such famous essays as "The American Scholar."

Notebook RT illustrates Emerson's long fascination with rhetoric and oratory and suggests that the topics were vital to him; that the gathering of information about them was going to be extensive enough for him; and that he needed to keep a clear record of his ideas on the topics. But, that is perhaps the least notable of a series of comprehensive statements Emerson makes on the topic of rhetoric and its power to shape a culture and a people. Several lectures and two published essays on the topic demonstrate that Emerson found rhetoric not only noteworthy but essential as well, and his persistent writing about it in journals and topical notebooks (which then emerge in truncated forms in his published essays) testifies to the fact that the study of rhetoric was an ongoing project, not a passing or subordinate interest. The point of this study is to uncover some of Emerson's explicit engagement with what we now call "rhetorical theory" in order to convey that rhetoric as an object of study was, in fact, central to his career.

Emerson, the Builder of Discourse

The idea of "eloquence" as a form of power derives from a history of ideas about language that extends beyond our preoccupation with Emerson as a literary artist, a prose stylist, a religious thinker, and a philosophical sage. Each of these roles and their disciplinary traditions illuminate Emerson's way of thinking about language as an instrument for social change, and each provides invaluable historical, theoretical, and social contexts for describing Emerson's work as a writer, orator, and thinker. The histories described by each tradition intersect with each other and expand to other fields, including poetics, logic, and science. At times, one becomes so deeply conflated with another that discerning precise lineages is hopelessly reductive, if not outright impossible.

That conflation, however, has obscured another history, a rhetorical history, of which Emerson was not only an observer but also an active participant, deliberately crafting statements on rhetoric, eloquence, and even oratory in response to both rhetorical history and his contemporaries.

Early in his life, Emerson described his work as belonging to the tradition of rhetoric:

> I see these truths chiefly in that species of architecture which I study & practice, namely, Rhetoric, or the Building of Discourse. Profoundest thoughts, sublime images, dazzling figures are squandered & lost in an immethodical harangue. We are fatigued, & glad when it is done. We say of the writer, "Nobody understood him: he does not understand himself." But let the same number of thoughts be dealt with by a natural rhetoric, let the question be asked—What is said? How many things? Which are they? Count & number them: put together those that belong together. Now say what your subject is, for now first you know: and now state your inference or peroration in what calm or inflammatory temper you must, and behold! out of the quarry you have erected a temple, soaring in due gradation, turret over tower to heaven, cheerful with thorough-lights, majestic with strength, desired of all eyes. (*JMN* 5: 409)

Emerson would have written these words the year before his infamous "Divinity School Address," in which he would argue against the highly stylized liturgies of the church, including its formalized (and to him spiritually empty) homiletics. The entry here shows that he is already expressing his desire for a natural or organic rhetoric, one that while methodical, escapes squandered figures and instead builds temples into the sky. *Rhetoric*, the "architecture which I study & practice," would be the term that helped bring together the various discourses that would shape Emerson's understanding of language and its impact on a society.

Throughout his career, Emerson returned time and again to rhetoric as an object of study and practice. Early in his life, he declared that he "hoped to put on eloquence as a robe" (*JMN* 2: 242), and when he first began lecturing, he imagined a new world opening before him and believed that the lecture hall would become the "true church of today" (*JMN* 7: 277–78). He would be among its first preachers, one who not only conveyed new truths but spoke in new ways and envisioned new possibilities for engaging an audience as well. He would repeatedly formulate what those new ideas and new forms of expression would be, and he would situate them under the general term of *rhetoric*, at times clearly choosing that term in opposition to other methods of knowing and acting in the world:

> I will not be chidden out of my most trivial native habit by your distaste, O philosopher, by your preference for somewhat else. If Rhetoric has no charm for you[,] it has for me[;] and my words are as costly & admirable to me as your deeds to you. It is all pedantry to prefer one thing that is alive to another thing which is also alive. The mystery of God inhabits a nursery tale as deeply as the laws of a state or the heart of man. (*JMN* 8: 402)

Emerson, as these statements imply and as the subsequent chapters of this study I hope prove, actively pursued rhetoric as an object of study. He theorized its importance and placed it in dialogue with, in equal measure, central figures in the history of rhetoric and nineteenth-century America.

Rhetorical Studies and Interdisciplinary Interventions

Any attempt to call Emerson a rhetorical theorist comes immediately upon two primary difficulties. The first is philosophical and the second is pragmatic. The philosophical issue derives from Emerson's ongoing (and well-documented) resistance to systemization. The rhetorical tradition, at least since Aristotle, has had a love affair with formal systems, and yet Emerson found them limiting and damaging. Literary scholars have long recognized that Emerson's rejection of forms and systems is at the heart of many of his projects as he attempts to reconnect ideas with expression. But while literary history often celebrates this feature of his work and of his prodigies' works, including, most obviously, Walt Whitman's poetry, rhetorical studies has failed to embrace Emerson's comparable call for a new rhetoric as a revolt against long-standing rhetorical systems. I address this feature of Emerson's work in two chapters. In chapter 4, "'*Habit* of Heat': Emerson, Belletristic Rhetoric, and the Primacy of the Imagination," I argue that Emerson upends American belletristic systems in order to forge a new rhetorical paradigm, and in chapter 5, "Emerson's Panharmonicon and the Sounds of a New Lecture," I describe Emerson's lecture career as an explicit repudiation of podium decorum.

The other difficulty is pragmatic, and that is trying to construct a coherent understanding of Emerson's vision of rhetoric from sources that are notoriously hard to corral. Emerson had two extended published statements on rhetoric, the first in 1870 and the second in 1875. Both are in the waning years of Emerson's career, a time when he was enjoying the status of the "Sage of Concord" and remaining largely settled in Concord, despite some notable trips, including one necessitated by a fire at his home. At this time, Emerson was also hard at work ensuring his legacy, just as his mind began to fade.

These late publications, however, are cobbled-together editorial constructions of the scattered lecture notes from his years in the podium. They collect sections of his lectures on "Eloquence" and "True Oratory" that he delivered from the 1840s to the end of his career. The lecture notes, which were eventually converted into essays, are held primarily in folders at the Houghton Library at Harvard University, in stacks of handwritten ruminations compiled into folders. The 1870 essay most resembles lecture notes from an "Eloquence" folder dated 1847 and comes from a lecture William Charvat calls Emerson's most popular. The 1875 essay is probably most closely related to an 1875 folder "Eloquence," but, as with the earlier essay, any attempt to draw a perfect textual correlation between the two is a fruitless endeavor. In addition to the 1847 and 1875 folders, there is an 1867 "Eloquence" folder that shares close connections with these essays and others. Beyond these published "essays," however, Emerson made comprehensive statements on rhetoric in other essays, some of which have received virtually no scholarly attention. Emerson's discussion of rhetoric in his lecture on Edmund Burke, which I examine in chapter 2, is the most notable among them.

The jumbled nature of the lecture folders is legendary among Emerson scholars. In *The Later Lectures of Ralph Waldo Emerson, 1843–1871*, Ron Bosco and Joel Myerson, two of Emerson's greatest and most careful textual champions, describe the complexity of their task and are quick to note the difficulties of their "transcriptions" of the lectures into published documents: "We must state that we have had to deal with texts far more fluid in their evolution and unstable in their preserved manuscript state than the texts in [collections of earlier lectures]" (1: xxxiv). They note that among Emerson scholars, common wisdom, shaped by editors of earlier lectures, was that lectures after the 1840s were too disorganized in manuscript form to be published, but that such "suspicion" was grounded on a failure to review the complete extant manuscript holdings, many of which could be "responsibly" edited for publication. They note that "the state of lecture manuscripts following 1871 that we inspected does, indeed, make impossible the preparation and publication of Emerson's lectures after that date in any coherent and responsible fashion," but that their project nonetheless collects nearly fifty lectures that, up until that point, had received little, if any, attention (1: xl). In mining the manuscripts, Bosco and Myerson have created new avenues for scholarly exploration, one of the chief ones being the examination of Emerson's ideas on lecturing, oratory, eloquence, and rhetoric. The confusion within the manuscripts need no longer limit, in this case, theorizing Emerson's impact on a field.

Nonetheless, the manuscripts still provide untapped resources, and sifting through them will remain, as it always has been, a laborious exercise. Emerson's method of composition was complex and, for textual historians, problematic; and the fact that Emerson crafted essays out of lectures has only heightened the difficulty of discerning how to read his work. Further, a clear sense of Emerson's project has been hampered because most of the scholarship on Emerson's mode of composition inevitably envisions his writing as primarily intent on essay production, leaving lectures as a kind of intellectual wayside, an unpleasant and incoherent interruption of the process from journal writing to essay composing. While Emerson certainly saw the essay as an important and even potentially revolutionary means of expression, he also viewed the lecture as potentially formative to a new American literature and a new American state. As Bosco and Myerson point out, "lecturing was significantly more than just a means to obtain money, more than a financially driven alternative career" (*Selected Lectures* xiii). Lecturing was, indeed, part of his own sense of vocation and provided means for the public dissemination of his ideas.

Certainly, any investigation of his composition must rely on the careful work of textual historians. Glen Johnson establishes that Emerson's characteristic prose style was, in fact, deliberate and had its sources in Emerson's lectures. Johnson argues that the lectures are essentially essays-in-the-making, and his side-by-side comparison of lecture and essay texts illustrates the changes Emerson made when moving from one genre to another. Nonetheless, his analysis assumes that the published essay was an uncomplicated or inevitable telos, as though the lectures were underdeveloped philosophizing. Scholars of oratorical culture, of course, will find in such side-by-side comparisons far different readings, whereby certain compression of diction within the text or Emerson's yielding to greater decorum illustrates his keen awareness of differences between auditors and readers. For example, the compression of text may be less about "improvement" of style, as some textual historians suggest, and more about various enthymemes that animate a lecture to a specific audience yet would be meaningless to a broad readership.

Johnson's work, nonetheless, recognizes that there is not only a deliberate set of changes but that those are also driven by Emerson's "adapting his [style] to the written medium" (62). His astute argument that "the final stage of revision is more strictly rhetorical, designed to serve the *communication* of meaning between artist and reader" (51) reminds us of Emerson's rhetorical inclinations, even if it also subtly suggests that Emerson's work was only complete (in its ability to communicate) when it reached essay form. Such preferencing of written expression over oral delivery undermines consideration of Emerson as primarily a lecturer whose method of composition may, in fact, have derived as much from a rhetorical heritage as a literary one.

More recent analysis of Emerson's habits of composition has followed the insistence that his lectures are primarily incomplete or practiced essays. For example, Paul Grimstad argues that Emerson's trip to Paris and his encounter with natural history cabinets of curiosity provided Emerson with an analogue for his written compositions. He contends that the arrangement of the cabinets inspired Emerson to see how juxtapositions and relationships within a cabinet could suggest new meanings and new ways of communicating the story of natural history. As a result, Emerson's style of lecturing and, ultimately, writing borrowed a cabinet-style organization. Accordingly, Emerson's style might be figured as a visual cabinet of artifacts, purposefully, if also surprisingly, arranged in order to communicate some greater truth about the object of discussion. Grimstad's position is provocative, and it provides a useful framework with which to see Emerson's writing, but his insistence that Emerson moved inevitably toward "his preferred medium of the essay" (24) dismisses the possibility that Emerson's lectures were not simply stages in a revisionary process but themselves final constructions of an aural, not visual, cabinetry. By rethinking the relationship of Emerson's lectures to his essays, we may uncover what Nikhil Bilwakesh has called Emerson's method of "decomposition," in which Emerson, relying on quotation as a primary means of communication, breaks apart previous writings and orations and reassembles them—much like a natural history cabinet—to compose new ideas and new visions of the world for his listeners.

Reconsidering this relationship will require renewed archival work and a return to Emerson's handwritten notes and papers. The difficulty of constructing an Emersonian theory out of such papers points us not only to the often-discussed shortcomings in our textual reconstruction efforts but also to shortcomings in our approaches to actually understand what the lecture manuscripts represent. Simply put, the study of his lectures demands that we take seriously that they were, in fact, artifacts of Emerson's deep study of rhetoric and oratory. Regardless of eventual transformations into essays, the lectures illustrate the very nature of what's at stake in his rhetoric in the same way that his essay manuscripts illustrate what is at stake in his essays. Emerson was a lecturer who was trying to revolutionize rhetoric and how it should function in the New Republic. If we understand that, we are forced to confront the idea that his lectures are deliberate repudiations of previous rhetorical systems, arranged not simply to confuse our essay reconstruction efforts but to forge new modes of ecstatic delivery.

It's striking that generations of scholars have wrestled with the contents of the manuscript folders as, for the most part, half-composed essays, often with simply a nodding acknowledgment that the essays were once lectures. Bosco and Myerson are a notable exception, emphasizing in recent anthologies the need to fully grapple with what lectures were in nineteenth-century America. Typically, however, we have spent a good many years examining the lectures as essays-in-the-making instead of lectures as rhetorical demonstrations. Our criticism, therefore, has tended to apply theories that circulate within fields focused on textual production—literary criticism, history, religion, and all manner of philosophical chatter. Bosco and Myerson call attention to the use of reader-response theory, noting especially the work of Sallee Fox Engstrom, and in doing so, they recognize the need for some sort of audience-focused approach to the work. However, no matter how useful the manuscripts are in understanding Emerson as a writer of prose, they primarily remain evidence of a career in the podium. As a lecturer, Emerson's writing and oratory come together, yet they are rarely considered on their own merits as rhetorical documents. Indeed, understanding them as lectures requires us to expand our approaches to his entire corpus. It requires us to look toward theories of invention, composition, arrangement, and expression from the field that has historically theorized the lecture and oratory: rhetoric.

Emerson's rhetorical ancestry has remained obfuscated by disciplinary divides, and we have given only cursory attention to him as a rhetorician. Even though early literary critics who helped secure Emerson's place in the canon of American literature recognized his engagement with oratory as a field of study, few developed any sustained vision of him as a rhetorician. F. O. Matthiessen noticed this long ago in his *American Renaissance*, and yet the idea has gained remarkably little traction:

> In declaring that the best prose becomes poetic, that the sublimest speech is a poem, Emerson was voicing the special desire of the transcendentalists to break through all restricting divisions. But in his tendency to link poets and orators whenever he listed the various arts, he was responding to a more common and widespread belief of his time.
>
> To a degree that we have lost sight of, oratory was then the basis for other forms of writing, and its modes of expression left a mark on theirs. (22)

Matthiessen notes that Emerson "defined a prose writer as 'an *orateur manqué*'" and points out that Emerson once declared American literature drew its power from rhetorical expression: "'The very finest and sweetest closes and falls are not in our metres, but in the measures of eloquence, which have greater variety and richness than verse'" (22). These observations lead Matthiessen to hyperbole, instructively so: "No American writer before Emerson had devoted such searching attention to his medium. . . . Emerson was concerned not merely with choosing his words and arranging them, but with probing to the origins of speech in order to find out the sources of its mysterious powers" (30).

The search for that power led Emerson, as I will argue, to central figures in what is now called the "rhetorical tradition," and if Matthiessen might now be less revered than he once was, he nonetheless points out a key feature of Emerson's work that has as yet still not been recovered—the ways in which rhetorical theory provided the basis for a theory of expression. Despite our ongoing engagement with Emerson as a thinker on any number of topics, we have not yet fully grasped the idea that rhetoric and oratory were often at the center of Emerson's conception of himself as a writer.

The reasons for this notable gap in research are varied and include several scholarly and disciplinary hurdles, among them an unspoken tradition of rhetorical studies that maintains nineteenth-century American rhetoric as simply the uncritical heir to the Scottish belletrists; the limited access until the last decade to central Emerson manuscripts on rhetoric; an ongoing (and ancient) view of "rhetoric" as a suspicious course of study; and, most notably, a long-standing disciplinary divide between literary and rhetorical studies that has sequestered important cultural figures into disciplinary camps. Thinkers like Emerson, Thomas Carlyle, and Harriet Beecher Stowe, for example, are effectively ignored within rhetoric curricula even as they remain prominent intellectual giants within literary studies. Similarly, literary scholars, due to their training and inclinations, have largely failed to consider rhetoric's impact on such figures—to consider them as descended of rhetoricians, not simply poets, prose stylists, literary writers, or philosophers. These writers, however, bridge our often rigid boundaries. All write explicitly about rhetorical theory. Accordingly, this book attempts to work across the disciplinary lines in order to make the case that broader consideration of Emerson's intellectual heritage provides richer, more nuanced, and, in some cases, more accurate understandings of Emerson's vocation and worldview. More importantly, understanding Emerson as a rhetorician helps us refine our approaches to theorizing nineteenth-century American public culture—its political orientations, its points of conflicts, and its simmering considerations of the relationship between individual freedom and civic duty.

Emerson does not, ultimately, fit neatly into a category—this has long been clear within academic debates as to whether he is a philosopher—and part of this project is to help demonstrate the limitations of situating him as solely literary or rhetorical artist. To understand him as either, one must look deeply into the influences of both. Nonetheless, this study leans more heavily on the rhetorical tradition, simply because that heritage remains the one that needs greater exploration. Literary scholarship runs deep and provides the most well developed examinations of Emerson's life, so placing him in a rhetorical tradition requires reliance on the work of literary scholars, whose invaluable insights into Emerson's composition, lecturing, textual habits, and surrounding culture form the foundation of today's Emerson criticism. Still, the rhetorical tradition is rich with its own history and its own vocabulary. Its theories emerge in ancient Greece and find expression throughout antiquity and into today, from ancient Rome, to medieval Europe, to the Renaissance, and into Emerson's America. Those theories have shaped conceptions of the spoken word and how it influences the written word and culture, and they figure language at the nexus of individual and social power. This study, then, aims to balance the ship a bit, not in the spirit of disparaging or denigrating one discipline's history and vision of Emerson's life and writings, but in the spirit of expanding a vision and locating him within a tradition that, despite its longevity and significance to American culture, has remained unexamined.

In short, this study is an attempt to secure a place for Emerson in the rhetorical tradition while reorienting his significance to literary history. Further, it is an attempt to collapse certain rigid disciplinary frameworks by describing points of contact between fields and establishing the ways in which Emerson himself conflated elements like rhetoric, writing, poetry, and eloquence. In order to do so, it juxtaposes Emerson with rhetorical theorists with whom Emerson "conversed." Emerson's range of reading on the topics of rhetoric and eloquence is breathtaking, and if we have stood in awe of his wide reading in literature from across the globe, we might similarly stand in awe of his engagement with rhetorical theorists. Our orientation toward the former has simply overshadowed our active pursuit of the latter, a habit that represents, in Emerson's terminology, "a foolish consistency" we would do well to break if only to enrich our own understandings of Emerson's world and nineteenth-century American culture.

This is not to make an exhaustive claim to finally "shedding light" on Emerson's "real" identity. Instead, this work aims at an intellectual archaeology, recovering a tradition with which Emerson was not only familiar but also widely conversant, but that has garnered relatively little attention. Rhetoric as a current of thinking within his work spans his career, from college to his final years as a lecturer—a time that accounts for nearly sixty years of the nineteenth century. By illustrating Emerson's ongoing fascination with various rhetorical theorists, this study hopes to initiate a new way of thinking about Emerson and prompt further exploration of rhetorical culture of nineteenth-century America. Emerson's view of both literature and rhetoric as distinct expressions of the imagination undoubtedly has unnoticed heirs, proponents, and ancestors, and this study's wish is that opening the door to readings of Emerson as a rhetorician will prompt new readings of other canonical figures as well as writers and orators who may have escaped notice because our disciplinary identities have limited broader understandings of Emerson's time.[1]

Chapter 1 of this study, then, examines Emerson's engagement with Plato's "true rhetoric" in order to demonstrate that Emerson's study of rhetorical history shaped his understanding of the public sphere. Emerson maintained a lifelong interest in Plato, and part of that interest included his consideration of Plato's theories of rhetoric. Emerson read both of Plato's key dialogues on rhetoric, as well as many others, and he takes from Plato the importance of connecting rhetoric with truth. In doing so, Emerson also finds in Plato an unlikely proponent of democracy, and

Emerson's project in reading Plato was, in part, to find ways for rhetoric to connect truth with civic good. Plato represents that possibility for Emerson, and he uses Plato to theorize a rhetoric that ensures democratic access to transcendence.

Emerson's surprising reading of Plato as truth-loving pluralist serves as a foundation for chapter 2, which argues that Emerson's love of the common man's native eloquence finds its ancestry in not only Plato and Cicero but Edmund Burke as well. Emerson repeatedly figures Burke as a modern-day Cicero, and he does so in order to demonstrate a theory of eloquence that valorizes the common man. In doing so, he both proffers an apologia for Burke's aristocratic opposition to the French Revolution and forges a rhetorical relationship between Cicero and Burke. Reimagining Ciceronian rhetoric, Emerson suggests that Burke represents a rhetorical theory that Americans can emulate.

Emerson's fascination with the common man has been widely examined, and in the last decade, the impact of Emerson's theory of the individual has taken a turn to suggest that his unique brand of individualism leads to a sense of resignation to higher order and, in the words of one commentator, corporate power. This "Emerson effect" has been well described in terms of socioeconomics and culture, but how it manifests in his language theory has been less thoroughly reviewed. Chapter 3 of this book suggests that Emersonian resignation has its roots in Augustinian hermeneutics and rhetoric. Arguing that Augustinian rhetorical theory presupposes a hermeneutic grounded in submission to the Word of God, it positions Emerson as an heir to this line of thinking whereby the rhetor persuades only when, after a hermeneutic act of analysis and reflection, he is absorbed into transcendental power. The result is a theory that bridges hermeneutics, rhetoric, and divinity.

While chapters 1 to 3 examine some of the larger figures in the history of rhetoric, chapters 4 and 5 take on two particular cultural phenomena that developed in nineteenth-century American rhetorical theory. The first is the influence of Common Sense philosophy and belletristic rhetoric on American schools of rhetoric. Most histories of American rhetoric rightly recognize the impact of belletrism on nineteenth-century instruction in rhetoric, and scholarship on the period's ongoing fascination with oratory and eloquence has demonstrated how work by belletrists like Hugh Blair provides a foundation for not just formal education but also more popular forms of oratory. Alternative histories have also circulated, finding new modes of expression in cultures as diverse as parlor room rhetorics, African American oratory, and Native American speech making, yet most of those rhetorical modes are sustained not by a coherent system of rhetoric as much as by a patchwork of examples that demonstrate certain preferences and ideologies underlying them. The scholarship is generally inductive, moving from example to general statements intended to give voice to unspoken theories circulating at the time, and it tends to formulate theoretical statements by observing cultural phenomena and not from specific or sustained textual evidence of a "rhetorical theory." Nonetheless, alternative theories that were explicit about their engagement with rhetorical history were extant in the nineteenth century, and one of those is Emerson's. Emerson deliberately positions himself as a foil to American belletrism, suggesting that the rhetoric of the imported Common Sense philosophy and the belletrists had become reified to a degree to be meaningless. Emerson criticizes American appropriation of belletrism more than the British work itself, and he argues that only through a more active exercise of the imagination can a new American rhetoric arise. This new rhetoric aims to overturn American lyceum propriety, resist systemization, and find new expression for some of the core ideals of British belletrist theory. Emerson, in short, posits an entirely new theory of rhetoric for the nineteenth century that has as yet not been fully recognized as a counterpoint to dominant modes of the time.

Emerson embodies this theory, both in his writing and in his speaking, and the final chapter of this book attempts to encourage more nuanced deliberation about Emerson's career as a lecturer. Previous examinations of Emerson's lecturing career have relied primarily on historical documentation through literary reception theories, and while such theories have been useful in positioning Emerson within a matrix of audience, culture, and text, they have left aside long histories of oratory and rhetoric. This last chapter suggests that the most compelling way to understand Emerson's lecture career is to put it in the context of a history of rhetoric and oratory, and it argues that only within that history can the full impact of Emerson's revolutionary rhetoric be felt.

These chapters, I hope, will persuade the reader that a vibrant history of rhetoric animates nineteenth-century expression and that Emerson is a central part of that history. If I can persuade the reader that that history is, itself, a central consideration of Emerson's career, all the better, but such a hope is not necessary to recognize that Emerson's expansive reading and thinking included both ancient and contemporary rhetorical theory and that his method of expression deliberately spoke to and, in some cases, rejected those theories.

That Emerson called for a new American literature has never much been in dispute, but that Emerson might have conceived of that literature as grounded in the discipline of rhetoric deserves more than passing recognition. Doing so will only confirm Emerson's fine-tuned thinking on the power of language to shape a society and, more broadly, the lasting impact Emerson made on the American scene. Indeed, I suggest it makes Emerson especially relevant now, in a time when writing instruction within our educational systems has been hijacked by those who would have us believe that language is nothing more than a standardized system of signs to be mastered or a set of lessons to be memorized and mimicked. Emerson never much liked imitation, and like Plato's true and only doctor, offers something like a remedy for such distortions.

1. "BEND TO IT OR DIE OF IT"

Emerson and the Democratization of Plato's "True Rhetoric"

Emerson's adoration of Plato began early in his life, and it hardly wanes as he ages. He finds Plato "best for what was intellectual and cosmical in the period" because he "taught an absolute unity" (*LL* 2: 233). Emerson's habit of regularly reading Platonic dialogues began before he matriculated at Harvard, and in 1822, at the age of nineteen, he concluded that Plato possessed two important characteristics: "intimate familiarity with the profoundest principles of philosophy, and at the same time a power to express them with the most perfect simplicity" (*JMN* 1: 148). Emerson's fascination with the connection between ideas and expression in Plato persists long after his time at Harvard. Just as he launches his career as a lecturer, Emerson immerses himself in a fervent examination of Plato's work. Library lending records indicate that Emerson borrowed Plato more than any other readings from the 1830s through the 1840s, and his own personal book collection grew to include multiple translations. Throughout the 1840s, he continuously maintained in his journals a section entitled "Platoniana" (*JMN* 10: 469–85), and by 1860, after his 1850s lecture series on *Representative Men*, he draws from that section while speaking in nearly rapturous language about the influence of Platonism on the life of the mind:

> No doctrine has shown more vitality in this way than what is called the Platonic Philosophy. . . . [P]ure power of thought clearing itself of the limits and traditions of the people, and trying its force on the problems of man and nature, with a courage and perception that yielded more memorable statements, more coherent particulars rounding into a theory of life and practice, than ever belonged to a movement which was essentially intellectual.

> . . . Plato's best for what was intellectual and cosmical in the period. It consisted in the affirmation of the mind as the source of all things; it taught an absolute unity. . . . All power, all good, all beauty, was in the mind. The soul, sufficient, could convert evil to good. Truth was the end and aim: he that had it was so far safe, immortal, and godlike. (*LL* 2: 233)

Such revelry is what leads early biographers, such as Phillips Russell, to declare that Emerson "sifted from Plato and Plato's mystic expounders" the idea that "at the core of all things, beneath their apparent differences in structure, lay an unbreakable unity" (40).

For critics like Russell, Emerson's transcendental idealism, which seeks an "Ineffable Oneness" (40) permeating the structure of the universe, is situated squarely within a history of philosophy, ontology, and epistemology. Platonism as a philosophical artifact and mysticism as a way of knowing encircle discussion of Emersonian transcendentalism, and Plato is figured as Emerson's ancestor within a long-standing history of ideas. In this formulation, Plato comes to Emerson not only through the Platonic dialogues but also through the Neo-Platonists, who lent to Emerson a sense of "ecstasy in which Neo-Platonism as a system of mysticism lives and moves and has its being" (Harrison 30).[1]

Emerson posits the centrality of language within that system, and while the history of philosophy yields essential touchstones for the relationship between language and the life of the mind, the history of rhetoric provides an equally vital heritage. Rhetorical history intersects with philosophical history and animates much of Emerson's work, and Emerson's focus on a Platonic rhetorical tradition manifests with significant force early in his career. Emerson uses Plato to unravel the relationship between the mind, the civic body, and language, and in doing so, he conceives of Plato as a "representative man" for American democracy. Plato, for Emerson, joined philosophy and rhetoric, and Emerson's conception of language, which is at the heart of his transcendentalism,[2] derives, in no small part, from Plato's rhetorical theory. While Emerson would adopt Plato as the father of a certain vein of mysticism that echoes throughout the treatises of the Neo-Platonists, he more importantly found in Plato a clear articulation of how civic action could be yoked with transcendence. Put more precisely, Emerson found in Plato's rhetoric a means of reconciling the life of the mind with the life of a citizen in the New Republic.

Emerson and Plato's Rhetoric

Emerson read Plato's core statement on rhetoric, the *Phaedrus*, repeatedly early in his career, including in 1841, just after he published *Essays, First Series* and was beginning work on his first "Eloquence" lecture (R. Richardson 346).[3] Though Emerson apparently read some ancient texts in Greek and Latin, including some of Cicero's orations, he preferred translations of Plato. According to Robert Richardson, "insisting on reading books in the original [languages] when translations were available seemed to Emerson perverse, like insisting on swimming the Charles River instead of taking a bridge to Boston" (284). He read extensively from Thomas Taylor's *The Works of Plato*, and in the 1830s and 1840s, at the heart of the time that he was first formulating a rhetoric, Emerson also read Plato from Victor Cousin's translations (R. Richardson 325).[4] Cousin, a prolific French philosopher who also wrote on Aristotle and Scottish Common Sense philosophy, enjoyed a considerable following in nineteenth-century America. His twelve-volume *Oeuvres de Platon* was well regarded among the intelligentsia of Boston, and Emerson's set (which covers Plato's central statements on rhetoric) was given to him by the Concord Lyceum (325).[5] Volume 3 includes *Gorgias*, Plato's scathing criticism of sophistry, and volume 6 includes the *Phaedrus*, Plato's fundamental reconsideration of rhetoric. Further, Cousin's set includes *Protagoras* (part of volume 3 with *Gorgias*) and *The Sophist* (volume 11), both of which engage with rhetoric as a shaping force in Greek culture. Emerson read from these dialogues throughout his career—Richardson calls it a "major preoccupation" for Emerson—returning to them frequently as source material for his lectures on Plato and on the power of language. Indeed, when Emerson finally formulates his first full statement on eloquence in 1847, he calls on Plato's definition of rhetoric in the *Phaedrus* to establish the grounds of his own argument. Emerson's invocation of Plato as the definer of rhetoric is important in and of itself, but that he calls on the *Phaedrus* is even more significant, as it establishes Emerson's line of argument that rhetoric is not simply "mere rhetoric" but that it can also be linked to transcendental truth (which is further discussed later in this chapter).

The *Phaedrus* is Plato's most developed discussion on rhetoric, and it comes twenty years after Plato systematically dismantles sophistic rhetoric in the *Gorgias*. In the *Gorgias*, Plato eliminates consideration of rhetoric as a "true art," and instead, in an infamous dismissal, describes it as a "knack." Even so, Rollin W. Quimby argues that despite

Plato's condemnation of rhetoric as a field of study in the *Gorgias* (indeed, Plato's point in the dialogue is that rhetoric is *not* a field of study at all), Plato nonetheless provides for the possibility of another rhetoric, one that evades the problems of sophistic oratory: "The passage [in the *Gorgias*] which excoriates rhetoric most harshly also contains hints that Plato has glimpsed the possibility of a 'good' rhetoric" (76). Quimby's reading is that Plato ultimately rejects the sophists and their failed philosophy more than the art of rhetoric itself. Similarly, Edwin Black, in his still standard assessment of Plato's "true rhetoric," argues that the *Phaedrus* is the "constructive complement" to the *Gorgias* that presents a "consistent view of rhetoric" as a "true art" that consolidates "dialectic with psychogogia" (91–92). This true rhetoric holds a basic "utility to the Ideal State" (99) that ensures knowledge and truth remain at the center of the act of persuasion: "Moral and metaphysical truths are to be rhetorically disseminated, not alone for the maintenance of political order, but so that they will be believed for their own sakes as well" (98). Quimby and Black both suggest, then, that the *Phaedrus* derives from an early examination of rhetoric in the *Gorgias* that shifts to an exploration of a more complex view of rhetoric and its relationship to truth and social order. Plato's condemnation of sophistic rhetoric in the *Gorgias* is simply groundwork for the articulation of a true rhetoric that could escape the dangers of sophistry and ascend to the status of philosophical art.

That the *Phaedrus* is concerned with the relationship between language, truth, and civic action is apparent when Socrates opens discussion of rhetoric in the dialogue. Socrates asks Phaedrus, "But what is rhetoric, what is left of it? That is the question that must be answered" (83), and Plato begins to condemn a false craft of rhetoric in order to contrast it with a true art that he will eventually outline. Socrates, speaking to Phaedrus, declares that "the existing writers of rhetorical manuals, whose lectures you have heard, are rogues: they are perfectly well aware of the truth about soul but choose to keep it from us" (91). The purveyors of this false rhetoric deceive an audience by misunderstanding the interaction between dialectic and expression, and they ultimately believe that simple devices can produce true conviction (87), a position which, for Socrates, undermines rhetoric's connection to truth.

A true rhetoric, however, is possible, and its purpose is "to influence the soul" (91). Socrates argues that those who seek merely for probability and rhetorical devices fail to search first for truth, through dialectic, as a foundation to rhetoric. "All the great arts," declares Socrates, "need to be supplemented by philosophical chatter and daring speculation about the nature of things" (89). True rhetoric, as James S. Murray suggests, requires philosophical speculation and a process of dialectical reasoning that "supplies the basis for the rhetorical art" (286). With truth as its ultimate goal and the movement of souls toward divine principles its purpose, persuasion elevates to a transcendental act. For Socrates, the resulting knowledge and its accompanying persuasion show "unity and plurality as they exist in the nature of things" (*Phaedrus* 82) and are necessary for the formation of a true rhetoric.

Socrates's requirement that a true rhetorician first engage in dialectic in order to discover "unity and plurality" echoes in Emerson's desire to reconcile "unity and variety" in the civic arena. If there is to be, for Emerson, a grand unification, it must be one that recognizes a plurality, one that can discern a shared harmony among the varying voices in the world.[6] He finds such possibility in a democratic theory of rhetoric, one that remakes Plato in order to ensure that truth, justice, and a transcendent unification remain at the center of discourse.

Emerson's Democratization of Plato

Certainly, Emerson's examination of the relationship between language and truth cannot be described as solely Platonic, nor is it solely rhetorical. James Warren, for example, argues persuasively that Emerson's early examination of eloquence derives from a desire to associate language with nature and a primal power that could only come from an Adamic, pure language source.[7] Warren's position highlights an ancestry of early language theorists that influenced Emerson's thinking, and it points toward the wide-ranging reading Emerson did as he wrestled with the relationship between language, democracy, and "things." That complicated relationship, however, is tackled most extensively by Stanley Cavell, who discusses not Emerson's reading habits but his influence on postmodern language theorists. Cavell's corpus on Emerson is, to put it mildly, itself wide-ranging, but much of his work is devoted to discussions of the idea that a philosophy of language is at the heart of Emerson's lifework. In his *Conditions Handsome and Unhandsome*, for instance, Cavell takes as a trope Emerson's declaration in "Experience" that he considers "the evanescence and lubricity of all objects . . . to be the most unhandsome part of our condition" (Cavell, *Conditions* 39). Cavell links this idea with a perpetual yearning toward moral perfection that is hemmed in by the limits of language to describe and enact our lives. He sees both the yearning and the limits as grounded in philosophical history:

> We may take for granted Plato's description of his task in the *Republic* as creating a "city of words," hence accept it that philosophy in the Western world unfolds its prose in a depicted conversation concerning the just city. Emerson's house of words is essentially less than a city; and while its word is not that of hope, its majesty is not to despair, but to let the "grandeur of justice shine" in it, and "affection cheer" it. (60)

Plato's and Emerson's language bridge the act of philosophical inquiry and the nature of philosophy itself, and Cavell's sense is that for Emerson, the just state is that which, perhaps evanescent itself, circles round the ineffable and yet gives voice to moral language, allowing justice to shine. The moral(izing) language, for Cavell, cannot be parsed out from other ways of describing and knowing the world, so that the moral, the aesthetic, or even the religious, join under the larger category of "philosophy itself" (61–62). In other words, philosophy is the exploration of the language used to describe and enact the moral imperatives we hold most dear.[8]

This constellation of thinking, from historical work like Warren's to philosophical work like Cavell's (which seeks not only to describe Emerson's project but apparently to embody it as well), spins around Emerson's ongoing consideration of the way that language, the self, and a society function together. Cavell, in particular, wants to associate Emerson's ideas on language with a striving toward democratic principles, and he does so not by distancing Emerson from Plato but by associating the two of them as parallel, if somewhat estranged, thinkers on the topics of philosophy and language. While the parallel is instructive, it also underplays Emerson's own project in reading Plato in order to rewrite his significance. That project amounts to nothing less than the reconciliation of Platonic idealism with democracy.

Emerson's 1850 essay "Plato; or, the Philosopher" democratizes Plato by imagining him as a philosopher whose primary virtue is his wedding of ultimate truth with social action.[9] Indeed, for Emerson, the idea of a philosopher, in general, requires that contemplation of divine or universal principles be yoked with civic duty, so that when Emerson reads Plato, he finds in him the greatest example of what a philosopher should be:

"Plato is philosophy, and philosophy, Plato" (*CW* 4: 23). By philosophy, here, Emerson means "the account which the human mind gives to itself of the constitution of the world," and at the heart of that account are two "cardinal facts": "unity" and "variety" (*CW* 4: 27).

Emerson links "unity" with divine and universal laws, and he relates "variety" with nature and the material world. For Emerson, this duality, quintessentially Platonic, demands the interconnectedness of both realms. Emerson does not declare the superiority of unity over variety. Instead, he argues that "it is impossible to speak, or to think without embracing both" (*CW* 4: 28). The idea that both unity and variety must be fully embraced is the foundation of what will ultimately be an attempt to reconcile Plato's essentialism with democracy.

That attempt is clear in his discussion on the ability of the mind to join the two concepts:

> These strictly-blended elements it is the problem of thought to separate and to reconcile. Their existence is mutually contradictory and exclusive; and each so fast slides into the other, that we can never say what is one, and what is not. The Proteus is as nimble in the highest, as in the lowest grounds,—when we contemplate the one, the true, the good, as in the surfaces and extremities of matter. (*CW* 4: 28)

Emerson, here, explores the problem that these two concepts appear contradictory, and he settles on the idea that it is the human mind that is made to reconcile their contradictions. John Holzwarth, who insists that Emerson's trademark optimism is generally misunderstood, describes how the diversity of experience squares with Platonic unity. He argues that, for Emerson, because "thinking is necessarily a subjective process, each of us has no choice but to rely on our own experiences; and because experience is the core ingredient of the intellect, intellectual potential is universal and not limited to a gifted few" (329). For Holzwarth, the subjectivity of experience makes it democratic, but the fact that subjectivity is a shared and universal experience moves it to a grander unity that requires respect for diverse viewpoints. If we accept that knowledge and expression derive from subjective experience and apply that principle to all people, then there is a shared ground on which to make claims: "It is because he [Emerson] remains ever conscious that one cannot grasp an impersonal idea [such as Truth] except by way of personal experience" (323). Emerson, then, "deepens and clarifies the arguments on behalf of democracy and individual freedom" (336).[10] Emerson's position suggests the possibility that Plato's own contradictions can be reconciled by the perceptive mind, and it provides him with a foundation on which to construct a Plato who will not be at odds with democratic variety, and thus, ultimately, rhetorical action.

Indeed, Emerson figures the twin principles of unity and variety as synonymous with a wide range of concepts that joins them with a life of action. "If speculation," he writes,

> tends thus to a terrific unity, in which all things are absorbed,—action tends directly backwards to diversity. The first is the course or gravitation of mind; the second is the power of nature. . . . One is being; the other, intellect: one is necessity; the other, freedom . . . one, possession; the other, trade: one, caste; the other, culture: one, king; the other, democracy. (*CW* 4: 29)

The contrast between king and democracy in the final pairing of the list is instructive because it stands as the culmination to a series of opposites whose ultimate purpose is the reconciliation of man with a polarized existence. For Emerson, the profound differences between monarchy, with a centralized authority, and democracy, where authority is shared between constituents, fade when the contrast is reconciled. Plato provides that reconciliation. Emerson argues that Plato yokes divine principle with earthly action in order to reconcile his own vision of the role of philosophy and language in the shaping of a society. Emerson's democracy is, after all, not the same as Plato's republic, but Emerson sees in Plato's work and life the possibility that universal law can somehow be connected to civic action.[11]

This is most apparent in Emerson's figuring of the geography of Plato's era. Emerson declares that "if the East loved infinity, the West delighted in boundaries" (*CW* 4: 30), and suggests that Plato reconciles East and West. After discussing the power of progress in science, technology, and politics in the West, Emerson writes that in the

> meantime, Plato, in Egypt and in Eastern pilgrimages, imbibed the idea of one Deity, in which all things are absorbed. The unity of Asia, and the detail of Europe; the infinitude of the Asiatic soul, and the defining, result-loving, machine-making, surface-seeking, opera-going Europe,—Plato came to join, and by contact, to enhance the energy of each. The excellence of Europe and Asia are in his brain. (*CW* 4: 30–31)

The contrast between the descriptions of Asia and Europe exemplifies the power Plato holds in reshaping the consciousness of man. It illustrates that "a balanced soul was born, perceptive of the two elements" (*CW* 4: 31) and that union of the extremes is possible. Emerson establishes Plato's role in bridging the two worlds in order to argue that the philosopher represents new possibilities for art and language in the New Republic, and he is careful to ensure that Plato appears not just as a sage but also as a common soul connected to all levels of society:

> If he made transcendental distinctions, he fortified himself by drawing all his illustrations from sources disdained by orators and polite conversers; from mares and puppies; from pitchers and soup-ladles; from cooks and criers; the shops of potters, horse-doctors, butchers, and fishmongers. He cannot forgive in himself a partiality, but is resolved that the two poles of thought shall appear in his statement. His argument and his sentence are self-poised and spherical. The two poles appear; yes, and become two hands, to grasp and appropriate their own. (*CW* 4: 31)

The catalogue highlights Plato's connection to the commonplace. It democratizes his language, suggesting that Plato's own words bridge the gap between the universal and the particular. Indeed, the movement from one space to the other distinguishes him and eventually provides Emerson with the idea that language, connected to the common and the democratic, gives universal access to truth.

This linking of the common with power is not unusual in nineteenth-century America or romanticism more broadly. Kenneth Cmiel argues that much of the cultural work of nineteenth-century orators was the bridging of high and low styles of language. The "middling style" combined the rude and lowly with the sublime and elevated in order to enact democratic power. Cmiel states that "the arrival of middling styles led to a war over the soul of American life" and that a "new vulgarity rudely challenged neoclassical notions about the morality of style" (66). Emerson was enamored with this possibility, and as Cmiel points out, "Emerson was captivated by the new popular literature of the 1830s . . . as he was by all sorts of vulgar speech" (113). Though Cmiel suggests that Emerson drifts toward gentility as he ages, Emerson nonetheless maintained a belief in the raw power of truth in the common man's words, and he found in Plato a kindred spirit in this belief: "the power and the charm of Plato" ("Plato," *CW* 4: 32), Emerson insists, derives from his ability to "build a bridge from the streets of cities to the Atlantis" (35).[12]

Central to Emerson's reading of Plato, then, is a project to make Plato a man of the streets (or, at least, someone who can speak meaningfully to the man of the streets) and a representative of democracy. Emerson does not deny Plato's essentializing; instead, he tries to reconcile it with the language of the "streets of cities." Understanding Emerson as involved in a project to democratize not only language but also Plato, the representative of truth seeking and idealism, clarifies precisely how rhetoric and philosophy, for Emerson, foster democracy.

Emerson's "Eloquence," True Rhetoric, and Democracy

Emerson's project to wed Platonism with democracy drives his rhetorical theory, but the requirement that rhetoric be connected to truth is precisely where some scholars, such as James Berlin, have limited the scope of Emerson's rhetorical theory. In *Writing Instruction in Nineteenth-Century American Colleges,* Berlin contests the idea that Emerson's rhetoric was Platonic, and he dismisses the scholarship connecting Emerson with Plato.[13] Berlin argues that positioning Emerson as a Platonist underestimates the complexity of Emerson's ideas and distorts his place in rhetorical history. He suggests that because Emerson must be described as working toward democracy, his rhetoric cannot be recognized as bringing truth through "internal apprehension" (43). Instead, truth is "organic" and grows "out of the entire rhetorical situation—reality, speaker, listener, and language" (57). For Berlin, Emerson is best understood as most closely related to "such moderns as Ernst Cassirer and Susanne Langer" because his works suggest that "reality is a human construction," with the "ideal by itself" a "meaningless abstraction" (45–46). In an attempt to secure Emerson's place in nineteenth-century American rhetorical theory and, more broadly, the rhetorical tradition, Berlin aligns Emerson with social constructivist understandings of the "self" and of the role of language in shaping it. He even suggests that Emerson's work rivals Aristotle's (57). In doing so, however, he mischaracterizes Emerson's project, which was in fact the reconciliation of Plato with a democratic rhetoric, the life of the mind with social action.[14]

While Emerson's rhetoric negotiates a set of principles that helps create and shape reality, speaker, and listener, Emerson never abandons the hope for a Platonic unity. Indeed, in outlining his rhetoric, he returns repeatedly to Plato for ideas on how rhetoric, truth, and civic action might all be reconciled into one system, finding in Plato both support for a true rhetoric and a condemnation of rhetoric that fails to live up to transcendental ideals. He writes about both the possibilities and the failures of rhetoric throughout his career, frequently invoking Plato's own theory.

Midway through "Plato; or, the Philosopher," Emerson acknowledges a particular debt to Plato in regards to rhetoric: "Socrates' profession of obstetric art is good philosophy, and his finding that word 'cookery' and 'adulatory art' for rhetoric, in the Gorgias, does us a substantial service still" (*CW* 4: 34). The reference is to Plato's condemnation of the art of rhetoric as a "knack," and it hearkens to a vision of rhetoric that questions whether sophistry can, in fact, be used in the service of truth. Here, Emerson, by aligning himself with Plato's statement in the *Gorgias*, seems to suggest that it cannot, but just as Plato would shift his discussion of rhetoric, so too does Emerson. He engages in the same search for a true rhetoric that is at the heart of Plato's *Phaedrus*, and he does so by aligning both rhetoric and Plato with democratic principles.

Emerson's inversion of the *Gorgias* occurs early in his career as he develops a nuanced, Platonic rhetoric. In an 1835 lecture on Michelangelo, Emerson joins beauty and art through a discussion of rhetoric and love that hearkens to the *Phaedrus*. He identifies Michelangelo as "a document or verification" of the "French maxim of Rhetoric, Rien de beau que le vrai; nothing is beautiful but what is true" (*EL* 3: 102). And he develops concepts of beauty, platonic love, and truth as central to Michelangelo's own expression, going so far as to cite one critic's respect for Michelangelo's writing in the face of bad contemporary poetry: "'He utters things; ye utter words'" (*EL* 3: 115). Similarly, in another lecture from the same series, Emerson praises Edmund Burke because his rhetoric inverts the idea that the term *rhetoric* is pejorative: "If the word Rhetoric had not by misuse acquired a hollow sound he [Burke] might be called a consummate Rhetorician, being a sort of artist or painter with words" (*EL* 3: 200). Emerson describes Burke as a person "who spoke to the world" and "espoused the cause of Liberty" by a rhetoric that "seeks to concentrate attention upon the facts but to consider them in accordance with the immense expansion in modern times of all the powers of society" (*EL* 3: 200–201). (See further discussion on Emerson's thinking about Burke in the next chapter.)

The distinction between "things," "words," and "society" was not, for Emerson, one that emphasized exclusion or preference; it was a distinction that demonstrated a necessary set of relationships that struck at the heart of how social order was created and maintained. In *Nature* (1836), the distinction is central to understanding the relationship between the human and the natural world, as well as the individual and the social sphere; and only a few years later, as Emerson ruminated on the need to reconcile individual action with social order, he turns to Plato for a solution. His notes for the 1839 lecture "Duty" cite the *Gorgias* and Socrates's position that only wisdom can guide the formation of a just society (*EL* 3: 441), and manuscript notes from 1831 demonstrate that he had considered the power of words far beyond simply signs of experience: "It is a common proverb that 'actions speak louder than words,' but it is only true when the words and the actions are at variance; when they are alike words speak louder than actions, are a higher class of actions. . . . Words are things or nothings" (bMs Am 1280.215, folder 134, p. 15).

Emerson's early reckonings with the effects of rhetoric on a culture lead to sustained discussions of rhetoric, eloquence, and the public sphere, culminating in his first extended statement on rhetoric in his 1870 "Eloquence" essay. The essay exhibits a profound reliance on Plato's rhetorical theory in its attempt to forge a new standard of eloquence for the United States.[15] "Eloquence" is one of two published works of the same name, one in *Society and Solitude* and the other in *Letters and Social Aims*. (The second "Eloquence" lecture and essay are discussed at length in chapter 4.) The one in *Letters* is derived from a lecture he gave at least ten times from 1867 to 1875 (*CW* 8: cclxiv), but the earlier one was, according to William Charvat, Emerson's most popular lecture. He began delivering it in 1847, and he continued using it, either in part or whole, even after he had composed and delivered the latter lecture. The frequency of delivery of both demonstrates the degree to which eloquence, rhetoric, and oratory were topics that were in demand on the lecture circuit.

The opening of the earlier "Eloquence," which is concerned almost wholly with the power of rhetoric to effect social change, highlights Emerson's project to bring rhetorical agency to all people: "It is the doctrine of the popular music-masters that whoever can speak can sing. So probably every man is eloquent once in his life" (*CW* 7: 61).[16] Emerson's positioning of all men as eloquent (a maneuver that highlights Cmiel's argument on the middling style) develops into an extended discussion on the results of this broad capacity of persuasion. He suggests that even the eloquence of one member of an assembly stimulates others either to come to the "speaking-point" themselves or become "good receivers and conductors" of his message so that when they "return to the fireside" they "avenge themselves for their enforced silence by increased loquacity" (*CW* 7: 61). In other words, the eloquent man either makes other men rise to great orations themselves, or he inspires them to conversation at their own homes. All listeners are made into eloquent speakers.

The opening of the essay, then, democratizes rhetoric, and Emerson, as a foundation for his polemic, calls on Plato to support his position:

> Plato says that the punishment which the wise suffer who refuse to take part in government, is, to live under the government of worse men; and the like regret is suggested to all the auditors, as the penalty of abstaining to speak,—that they shall hear worse orators than themselves. (*CW* 7: 62)

Emerson's analogy that compares silence in government affairs with silence of auditors highlights the power that Emerson assigns rhetoric. Rhetoric gives individual access to power, and that power is the right of all people. As he says in the following line, "but this lust to speak marks the universal feeling of the energy of the engine, and the curiosity men feel to touch the springs" (*CW* 7: 62). Rhetoric means access to universal power that is the right of all people, and for Emerson, Plato is evidence for that right to access.

Emerson's use of Plato moves beyond analogy, however, when he explicitly invokes Plato's theory in order to demonstrate the formative power of rhetoric: "Plato's definition of rhetoric is," Emerson writes, "'the art of ruling the minds of men'" (*CW* 7: 64). This line comes within a larger discussion of Emerson's own definition of rhetoric, and it shows Emerson's explicit engagement with Plato's rhetorical theory. It suggests that Emerson was adapting Plato to articulate a vision of rhetoric applicable to nineteenth-century America, and it illustrates that Emerson's appropriation of Plato was not simply an unexamined absorption of Platonic dualism—it was an attempt to redefine Plato in terms that broadened rhetorical agency in order to articulate a new true rhetoric.

As the passage continues, the remaking of Plato by Emerson becomes clear; he uses Plato to demonstrate the right to eloquence of all people:

> The Koran says, "A mountain may change its place, but a man will not change his disposition;" yet the end of eloquence is—is

> it not?—to alter in a pair of hours, perhaps in a half hour's discourse, the convictions and habits of years. Young men, too, are eager to enjoy this sense of added power and enlarged sympathetic existence. The orator sees himself the organ of a multitude, and concentrating their valors and powers:—
>
> "But now the blood of twenty thousand men
> Blushed in my face." (*CW* 7: 64–65)

The juxtaposition of Plato's definition of rhetoric with the Koran and the persuasive power of eloquence highlights Emerson's project. The Koran's wisdom, which suggests the ultimate stability of a core sense of self, is overturned by a Platonic definition of rhetoric, which proposes the possibility of change. The mutability of the listener, who is capable of making significant shifts in perspective, emphasizes Emerson's vision of a democratic rhetoric. It suggests that while Emerson wants to maintain a transcendental truth, he also wants to explore the possibility that language has the ultimate power to move people to that truth through forging their dispositions.

Real rhetoric, then, is akin to the true rhetoric that Plato describes in the *Phaedrus*. Its purpose is the movement of the soul to the divine, and its uniqueness is that its breadth of power is not limited to an elite class. Emerson calls it "transcendent eloquence" (*CW* 7: 92), and he compares the man who is capable of producing it to a guide:

> In every company the man with the fact is like the guide you hire to lead your party up a mountain, or through a difficult country. He may not compare with any of the party in mind or breeding or courage or possessions, but he is much more important to the present need than any of them. (*CW* 7: 86)

Emerson's analogy significantly places the eloquent man as a common man, one who may be of lower breeding but who nonetheless has the right power at the right moment. He is a guide precisely because he knows a special territory, and that knowledge and connection to "fact" has very little to do with class. It is a broad power, and in any given moment, a guide from any background can rise to provide a special power to overcome the profoundest obstacles.[17]

Equally important, all people are susceptible to the power of the eloquent speaker. Indeed, eloquence is capable of converting men to truth even if they would attempt to resist it:

> There is for every man a statement possible of that truth which he is most unwilling to receive,—a statement possible, so broad and so pungent that he cannot get away from it, but must either bend to it or die of it. Else there would be no such word as eloquence, which means this. The listener cannot hide from himself that something has been shown him and the whole world which he did not wish to see; and as he cannot dispose of it, it disposes of him. The history of public men and affairs in America will readily furnish tragic examples of this fatal force. (*CW* 7: 91–92)

In a remarkably Platonic move, Emerson here describes an unveiling of truth that is impossible to resist. The auditor who hears a profound truth has a choice to either embrace that truth or be undone by it. It attacks his very being and forces him to change. For Emerson, America provides fertile ground for examples of the power of this eloquence. Indeed, America seems to be the special location for this type of transcendental eloquence.

Emerson and the Promise of a Transcendental Rhetoric

Emerson imagined a distinctly American transcendental rhetoric as formative to the new American state. To Emerson's mind, an opportune moment had arisen in the history of humanity, and a special rhetoric would be necessary to speak for that time.[18] For Hans von Rautenfeld, that new Emersonian rhetoric is representative, and it ensures that democracy maintains a vibrant public sphere: "For Emerson what makes an utterance 'public' is not its location, but its representative nature, which means that it is offered not as an individual expression without claim to general acceptance, but with the reasonable expectation that it could be accepted by others" (185). Moreover, while representatives collect and speak for various communities, they also participate in those communities and become audiences themselves, who are then represented by others, so that "as a polity becomes more democratic, its public sphere becomes at once more inclusive (and more participatory) and more mediated (and less direct)" (185). In other words, as some individuals rise to represent common concerns, they also mediate those concerns when they communicate them. Von Rautenfeld notes that Plato for Emerson "exemplifies" the representative of a democracy because "he devises unity and produces connections, correspondences, and relations among individual selves severally and between the community of individuals and the diversity of things" (189). The result for von Rautenfeld is that Emerson mediates his individualism because he "worries that 'an inflamed individualism' will prevent individuals from connecting with their communities" (190). Emerson's rhetoric, then, is transcendental because as a representative force, it moves beyond individual concerns to a representation of shared concerns between diverse constituents of a community.

Emerson's formulation of a transcendental rhetoric has been frequently read as dangerously individualistic and profoundly destructive to certain aspects of American culture. Indeed for some, Emerson's theory is responsible for the demise of the study of rhetoric as a distinct discipline. For example, W. Ross Winterowd argues in two different venues that Emersonian rhetoric, through its insistence on quietism and idealism, essentially helps to dismantle rhetoric as a field of study in the United States. For Winterowd, Emerson's idealism leads to solipsism, and he maintains that Emerson's romanticism, with its attendant Platonic dualities, is the root of an often-described crisis in rhetoric and composition studies in the late eighteenth and early nineteenth centuries.

Winterowd's position is articulated in some central venues in the discipline of rhetoric and composition, including in *A Teacher's Introduction to Composition in the Rhetorical Tradition* (with Jack Blum), a text intended for use in instructing teachers of composition about the role of rhetorical history on the discipline of composition studies. Implicitly contesting Berlin's position that Emerson's theory is social, Winterowd's work argues that Emerson is destructively Platonic and that he removes traditional notions of audience from rhetorical theory.[19] With the concept of audience eliminated from language use, the idea of genuine dialogue and, by extension, democracy is impossible. Winterowd, however, does not account for Emerson's larger project. Like Berlin, he fails to see Emerson's desire to reconcile Platonic idealism with the question of "how to live" and thus also fails to see how Plato is figured as necessary to the democratic ideal.

Emerson's work shows an ongoing fascination with how to move away from *quietism* (the word Winterowd uses to describe Emerson's fascination with a Platonic sense of self and contemplation) and toward ethical action. The most obvious example is Emerson's "American Scholar," which explicitly repudiates the quietistic "bookworm" in favor of a vision of the scholar as a man of action, but Emerson's work on Plato and eloquence also clearly illustrates this concern. When Emerson reconciles Platonism with a life of action, he does so in order to embrace the possibility that rhetoric can shape an audience and change a society. That he relies on transcendental truth as a foundation for his argument does not inherently require Emerson to move away from the civic power of rhetoric. Such a reading of Platonism fails to account for the project that Emerson was undertaking, and it fails to account for the historical moment of transcendentalism in general.

Winterowd's assessment brings to Emerson's essays a reading of Plato derived from a very specific set of cultural critiques that presumes that nineteenth-century readings of the ancient Greeks mirror current readings. Emerson's and many of his peers' readings of Plato, however, make very different assumptions about Plato because of specific historical contingencies. Emerson was trying to find a place for Platonic idealism in the shaping of a young country, and in doing so, he reconfigured what today might seem to be irreconcilable dualities. For Emerson the split between the spiritual world and the material did not implicitly prioritize one domain over the other. Instead, Emerson negotiates the terrain between the worlds and suggests, ultimately, that language and action were means of straddling them and realizing real change in society.

Randy Friedman argues that a "strand of pragmatism" in Emerson "*depends* on certain metaphysical commitments," and that "the traditional reading of Emerson as anti-religion, and by extension, anti-religious, impedes a better understanding of self-reliance" (154). For Friedman, Emerson's "democratic tendencies, or, what makes him a democrat, is his pluralistic metaphysics," and he points out that William James called Emerson "'the philosopher of democracy'" because he "emphasize[s] metaphysical intimacy and oneness with an unseen order" (156). Friedman's project is to recover Emerson as initiator of a vein of pragmatism in which "there is something, some type of intuition or moral sentiment in play" (178) that has been lost in the study of Emerson's philosophy. Doing so weds Emerson's moral sentiment with civic action. While Friedman locates that sentiment in a nascent American pragmatism, its roots are in Emerson's Platonism. For G. Borden Flanagan, Emerson's vision of democracy "draws on the Greeks, and on Plato in particular" (417), and Emerson invokes a "Platonic ontology" in describing a vast unity that is shared by all individuals. That unity embraces a radical diversity, and Emerson comes to embody, as one commentator has noted, "the nation's first democratic intellectual" (Field 469). Ultimately, Emerson suggests the limitations of a simplistic view of Platonic selfhood while highlighting the possibilities of broad action in the world. Rhetoric, for Emerson, is at the center of the thoroughfare of action because it provides the means through which participation in social change can be prompted. Emerson's theory of rhetoric relies on Plato's conception, but Emerson deploys Plato in order to argue that rhetoric both embraces the search for transcendental truth and democratizes language use. The core of "Eloquence," in particular, is Emerson's redefining a true rhetoric that is simultaneously democratic and Platonic.

Criticism that either dismisses Emerson's Platonism or reads Platonism as a static set of principles does so only by reading the work in light of current theories that minimize the possibility that the concept of Platonism is, in itself, culturally constructed. Such insistent and long-standing misrepresentation has been commented on even before recent readings of Emerson and Plato, perhaps most lucidly by Stuart Brown more than sixty years ago: "Platonism has been interpreted for us for more than a hundred years in the light of that German idealism which was secondary in Emerson's thinking and reading" (336), and that failed to account for Plato's shift, in Brown's mind, from monist to dualist. Emerson weds this later Platonism with democracy, imagining Plato as a common man whose conception of language squared tightly with the ideals of the New Republic.

To understand Emerson's position on Plato, then, requires an understanding of how Emerson (indeed, probably most of the transcendentalists) read Plato. We have such evidence from early in his life until later. His reckonings with Plato in his lecture on the philosopher demonstrate Emerson's exaltation of a democratized Plato, but he also finds later in his life that American culture displays a special readiness for the messages of Platonism:

> Now everything comes round, and so must Plato. After these great luminaries have had their age, have past [*sic*] away, and the poor world has quite forgotten them[,] . . . and we thought the old men and schools were buried once and for all,—here rises, in the last century, a scholar who sets them all on their legs again, gives them all an English tongue, and calls all the millions who can speak it to hear the wonderful discourse of these sages who lived and taught fifteen hundred years ago. (*LL* 2: 234)

Embedded in this pronouncement is Emerson's advocacy for the special work of the scholar, and it implies that Plato, speaking across ages, is resurrected on behalf of an age that can hear his message. Because more contemporary readings of Plato inevitably imagine him as he's understood today, the broader, nineteenth-century social project of reading him has been lost, one that locates in the figure of Plato an authority to claim democratic rhetorical power. The resulting theory participates in a tradition of rhetoric that seeks a true rhetoric and posits truth as requisite for moral change in society because it is accessible to all people. This accessibility provides, in Emerson's estimation, hope for the study of rhetoric because it implies that language is capable of effecting broad social change. Like Plato in the *Phaedrus*, Emerson theorizes a rhetoric whose function is the formation of a just society.

2. EMERSON, BURKE, AND THE LIMITS OF CICERONIAN ELOQUENCE

In the final paragraphs of a little known early lecture, Emerson offers a taxonomy of eloquence. He divides eloquence into three types—natural, practical, and philosophical—and he elevates the philosophical to a special sphere of influence. Given Emerson's preoccupation with Plato, as discussed in the previous chapter, his maneuver here comes as little surprise. He envisioned the philosophical mind as proactive and capable of shaping a society, not simply as immersed in contemplation or removed from the cares of the world. What is surprising, however, is the context of Emerson's taxonomy and its absence from scholarship on him as lecturer and rhetorical theorist. The lecture, "Edmund Burke," provides not only Emerson's first sustained statement on eloquence and rhetoric but also his most direct. It is his first attempt at theorizing a rhetoric, and it establishes a foundation of ideas that appear with increasing force and nuance in future work. Indeed, Emerson's endorsement of a revised Platonic true rhetoric finds its first expression in this lecture, and equally important, Emerson's assertion that the "common man" speaks with eloquence shapes his first sustained consideration of the role of rhetoric in a democracy.[1]

In January 1835, Emerson embarked on his first ever lecture series. Though he had given other lectures as his career as a preacher came to an end, his series on "Biography" marks his first, interrelated body of lectures. The series had been requested by the Society for the Diffusion of Useful Knowledge in Boston, and as the editors to *The Early Lectures* note, Emerson, at the time, was thinking broadly about both the lecture as a form and the lyceum as the location for delivery. (See chapter 5 for further discussion of Emerson's concerns with the lyceum.) While public lectures within the lyceum typically focused on science and practical knowledge, Emerson, as Stephen Whicher and Robert Spiller point out early in the history of Emerson scholarship, rapidly grew weary of that focus. Instead, Emerson yearned to draw connections, to find signs of greater patterns within the natural world and even the progress of the American state. This is not to say he viewed the world as a set of mysterious, preordained systems that simply had to be uncovered in order to be understood. Instead, Emerson aimed to forge the connection, to discern a unity that would give meaning to science, natural history, and the practical crafts of statehood.

Whicher and Spiller astutely recognize this yearning in Emerson's confrontation with the strictures of the lyceum, noting Emerson's early desire to break from it: "'I would learn the law of the diffraction of a ray because, when I understand it, it will illustrate, perhaps suggest a new truth in ethics'" (*EL* 1: 93). More importantly, they draw attention to Emerson's admonition to himself, as he prepares to give his first lecture series, not to simply parrot the scientific or historical findings of other thinkers and writers but instead to draw the connections between the facts he has learned and the lessons he finds most significant:

> "Henceforth," he vows on November 15[, 1834], just after he had moved to Concord, "I design not to utter any speech, poem or book that is not entirely and peculiarly my work. I will say at public lectures, and the like, those things which I have meditated for their own sake, and not for the first time with a view to that occasion." (*EL* 1: 93)

Emerson scholars will recognize in this passage the sentiment Emerson more forcefully asserts in "Self-Reliance," when he enjoins listeners and readers to speak their own minds, even if they fear being misunderstood. In the now famous passage, he insists that speaking with earnest conviction frees the speaker from concerns with "foolish consistency" or undue shackling of thought by the past:

> A foolish consistency is the hobgoblin of little minds, adored by little statesmen and philosophers and divines. With consistency a great soul has simply nothing to do. He may as well concern himself with his shadow on the wall. Speak what you think now in hard words, and to-morrow speak what to-morrow thinks in hard words again, though it contradict every thing you said to-day.—"Ah, so you shall be sure to be misunderstood."—Is it so

> bad then to be misunderstood? Pythagoras was misunderstood, and Socrates, and Jesus, and Luther, and Copernicus, and Galileo, and Newton, and every pure and wise spirit that ever took flesh. To be great is to be misunderstood. (*CW* 2: 33–34)

Emerson's early insistence "not to utter any speech . . . that is not entirely and peculiarly my work" finds fuller expression in "Self-Reliance" as he extends his self-admonition to public exhortation. He assures his listeners that even if contradictions appear and misunderstandings emerge, they need not fear that these flaws have violated audience expectations. Instead, a deeper pattern may emerge, one which will vindicate the honest expression of the moment:

> There will be an agreement in whatever variety of actions, so they be each honest and natural in their hour. For of one will, the actions will be harmonious, however unlike they seem. These varieties are lost sight of at a little distance, at a little height of thought. One tendency unites them all. The voyage of the best ship is a zigzag line of a hundred tacks. See the line from a sufficient distance, and it straightens itself to the average tendency. Your genuine action will explain itself and will explain your other genuine actions. (*CW* 2: 34)

Emerson's recourse here to a sense of grand unity is unsurprising, but the nature of it as being corroborated by time and perspective suggests that when Emerson talks about the effects of language, he isn't simply considering the effects of words on an individual. Instead, Emerson here places the speaker in the context of a public, one that listens skeptically, concerned always with the logical contradictions and inconsistent particularities of each moment. The speaker's role, in this instance, is not to challenge the audience, demand closer attention, or turn to apology or explanation. The speaker instead trusts that the "zigzag" will straighten out with time and perspective, that the hard words spoken will demonstrate a greater continuity and more genuine path for social improvement.[2]

This "Self-Reliance" passage is typically read as exceedingly internal, even if paradoxically so. Jonathan Bishop observed decades ago that the structure of the essay relies on paradoxical juxtapositions between an inner soul and an outer providence in order to highlight the impact of the individual in the world (92–97), and George Kateb suggests that Emerson's sense of self-reliance is profoundly individualistic while avoiding the self-centeredness of "mean egotism." Kateb calls this "democratic individuality," and he argues that "self-reliance is thus not a doctrine of superiority to average humanity. Rather it is a doctrine urging the elevation of democracy to its full height, free of the aristocratic, but also free of the demotic" (18). Regardless, the significance of the passage is that it places the individual in context with a crowd, with those he might persuade. Emerson asks his audience members to "speak," to say their innermost convictions in an attempt to help usher in what he calls at the end of another essay, "a nation of men" that "will for the first time exist, because each believes himself inspired by the Divine Soul which also inspires all men" (*CW* 1: 70). While most scholarship focuses on Emerson's preoccupation with the "self" in the passage, especially as it relates to the creation of a distinct voice in American letters, the text's echoing of Emerson's early thinking on how he might himself approach the lectern suggests that the passage also embodies Emerson's vision of a new kind of orator. He is, after all, dramatizing the passage through appeals to public speaking. In other words, Emerson's insistence on "speaking" hard words applies not only to philosophers and divines but also to statesmen—the first in his list of "little" minds. This is a statement on rhetoric, if also individualism, metaphysics, or belles lettres, and its invocation of statecraft echoes in Emerson's appraisal of the great statesman Edmund Burke.

"Edmund Burke," Virtue, and Democracy

Emerson begins his "Edmund Burke" lecture with a decidedly dry series of biographical observations about his subject. He notes Burke's birthplace and year, favorite writer (Plutarch) and orator (Demosthenes), and then moves into a brief timeline of his public service. The factual orientation of the lecture contrasts rather sharply with some of the earlier lectures in the series, which begin with discussions of particular themes or grand visions, such as the opening of his lecture on Michelangelo, which focuses on the idea of harmony, or the lecture on George Fox, which starts with an ongoing rumination on "universal principles" in biography and how they do (and do not) apply to Fox. The opening of the Burke lecture, however, seems obsessed with detail, and the quantity of accomplishments and feats of statesmanship that marks Burke's career. Indeed, Emerson's fixation on the "variety of this man's accomplishments" stands in contrast to the way in which the other lectures illustrate some singular feature of the figure under examination. The Burke lecture, the closing of the series, moves away from the pattern of organization that marks the earlier lectures.

Part of this might be attributed to the fact that, until just weeks before the lecture, Emerson himself had apparently not yet decided on the subject of the final lecture. Whicher and Spiller cite journal and notebook entries testifying to the fact that Emerson had been planning to speak on the other figures in the series (Michelangelo, Luther, Milton, and Fox), and they note that only a couple of days before the lecture, he had been intensively reading Burke biographies (*EL* 1: 183). They suggest that Emerson's development of the speech was late, even though they point out that Emerson had for some time been thinking about Burke as a "philosophical statesman." His journals show that he continued to link Burke with preeminent thinkers throughout his life. For example, in his fifties, he links Burke with Pindar to highlight the strong sense of play he felt when reading Burke's oratory: "I see the selfsame energy & action in a boy at football, that I admire in the intellectual play of Burke or Pindar" (*JMN* 14: 132). More importantly, he explicitly associates Burke with powerful rhetoric throughout his career. In one of his "Encyclopedia" notebooks he repeatedly quotes Burke under the subheading "Rhetoric" (*JMN* 6: 85), and later he describes Burke as the perfect model of rhetoric itself: "Burke is a rhetoric[,] a robe to be always admired for the beauty with which he drapes facts as we love light or rather colour which clothes all things. What rich temperance, what costly textures, what flowing variety" (*JMN* 7: 235).

The nature of the shift in organization of the Burke lecture, then, seems purposeful even if it might be read as residue of poor preparation—as Emerson scrambled to cobble together relevant notes to make a coherent vision. Emerson, nevertheless, had given much thought to Burke and Burke's oratory. Even so, the shift illustrates the very point that Emerson will make as the lecture develops, which is that Burke cannot simply be understood as the sum of his parts, that he represents a great unity that, though imperfectly realized, embodies an ideal speaker and statesman.[3] Burke represents both, and the lecture suggests the necessary interdependence of the two.

Edmund Burke is typically figured as a political conservative whose position against the French Revolution placed him on the wrong side of history. But Burke, as Emerson points out, was a supporter of American democracy or, at the very least, a representative government that encouraged public political activity by individuals of all backgrounds. As Stephen Browne argues,

> by stressing the virtue of political action, the author [Burke] gives his request [to participate in political action] a moral incentive; by reminding the reader of the power of the individual voice, Burke encourages confident resolve. Thus he posits an ideal reader and invites his actual audience to become this ideal. . . . [His] remarks locate "the people" (the reader) as the authorizing source of legitimate political action. (17)

Political action, linked for Browne to a concept of virtue, necessitates not dogmatic assertion of ideals, nor passive acceptance of claims to moral rectitude, but instead rests on a "collaborative" action between orator and audience, writer and reader (12).

Christopher Reid points out that this leads Burke to aligning rhetoric with moral thought and action. Rhetoric "is the mode in which thought is energised and in which philosophy is translated into action" (qtd. in Browne 81), but as Paddy Bullard points out, Burke insists that "the speaker depends on the generosity of the audience to distinguish his general good intentions (which can only be taken on trust) from the exigencies of his argument" (7). For both Reid and Bullard, this suggests a kind of dialectic between audience and speaker in which the speaker invites participation and the audience invites political guidance. Only when both speaker and audience work together, however, can effective persuasion and political action occur. In other words, if ethos, as Bullard points out, is of prime concern to Burke, it is an ethos in relation to an active and discerning audience. Ethos alone is not persuasive; it simply provides the speaker the opportunity to invite the audience to share in a moment of transformation. Reid contends that Burke absorbed this idea from Cicero, who believed that "the orator's capacity to be himself moved (through willed identification with a cause or as the first audience of his own words) was understood as a precondition of this transfer of emotion and consequently of persuasion itself" (48).

This orientation to rhetoric, which situates the effectiveness of oratory and writing within a shared experience between rhetor and audience, appeals to Emerson. Moreover, it reveals how Emerson attempts to reconcile his perhaps-overstated individualism with his sense of civic responsibility. Emerson finds in Burke the grounds for a rhetoric that, on the one hand, invites participation from all parties involved in a question and, on the other hand, avoids the pitfalls of the mob, which constantly threatens to undermine virtue by appealing to the lowest instincts of individuals.

As Emerson begins to develop his argument about Burke, he insists that Burke occupies a special place in history: "No single mind since Plato has enriched his fellowmen with so many of those truths which by their dignity and extent of application we incline to call laws" (*EL* 1: 187). Burke's rarified position results from his ability to yoke a philosophical life with an active life in the public sphere. Emerson argues that while Marcus Aurelius, Francis Bacon, and Machiavelli all approached the ideal, none was able to bring the philosophical life to public service. Aurelius, Emerson asserts, was not so much a philosopher as a "moral speculator"; Bacon abandoned philosophy when he joined politics and left behind "nothing valuable and much that is disagreeable to remember"; and Machiavelli's realm of influence was, in one of Emerson's more striking claims, "too small to be taken into the account of European history" (*EL* 1: 186–87). While Emerson insists that Bacon's philosophical writings are superior to Burke, he is concerned in this lecture with the political life and the ability to effect social change, and in that, "the advantage is forever with Burke" (*EL* 1: 188).

For Emerson, Burke's brilliance derived from his ability to discern meaningful patterns from facts. While he was "never a philosopher in the highest nor in the lowest use of that term," he was the "*philosophical politician*" who through "mental activity quickened and arranged without transforming every fact, every event. Things fell in his mind into associations of a new and natural kind. That which he saw disordered, assumed order in his own thought" (*EL* 1: 189–90). He accomplished such an ordering "without misrepresentation or neglect of any parts" (*EL* 1: 190) by taking "facts as the base" and reducing them "by the illumination of his genius into the best order which they themselves admitted, and, as it always seemed when he announced it, a natural and perfect order" (*EL* 1: 190). In short, Emerson saw Burke as a great synthesizer of information who could discern patterns amidst the chaotic facts of life.

Emerson recognizes that his description of Burke connects him to a "royalist" and "conservative" tradition, one that values order, coherence, even certainty in the face of the disruptive influences of "radical Reformers" and "revolutions," but he addresses Burke's conservative leanings with an apologia that connects rhetoric and ethics. Emerson argues that three particular traits explained the contradiction that Burke, as a conservative, would yet support democracy in a developing new world. The first is Burke's adherence to principles of Taste, which is discussed in more detail in chapter 4. For Emerson, "Taste is pacific; the objects on which it is conversant only collect themselves in quiet and stable communities" (*EL* 1: 190–91). Those objects, such as belles lettres and eloquence, only emerge in peace, and so his inclination toward taste, illustrated by his teaching oratory to the painter James Barry, predisposed him toward stability and the sublime arts that emerge from it.

Second, Emerson notes that Burke's own "attachments" kept him from moving from political philosophy to reform. Emerson spends several pages of his lecture describing the personal relationships, both familial and political, that Burke had formed throughout his life, describing him as a doting father and a sincere friend: "The affectionate, childlike sweetness of this man's temper which endeared to him his friends, his neighbors, his countrymen, naturally inclined him to take favorable views of the laws and the historical institutions of the state" (*EL* 1: 193). These attachments, which Emerson lists with reverence and admiration, eschewing condemnation of what others might consider simply self-interest, are the point on which Emerson pivots to connect Burke to a special kind of rhetoric that found footing only in new democracies.[4]

Emerson highlights the fact that Burke supported "the Americans" in their struggle against "oppression by the Crown" by suggesting that Burke's position represents a continuity of his thinking that was best exemplified by his advocacy for the "East Indians," for whom he "never ceased to fill the House with his indignation and entreaty until at last the Governor was impeached and the opportunity given him to open the whole enormous history of Indian tyranny" (*EL* 1: 195). That Burke fought against the French Revolution meant simply that he fought for established traditions within France, as well as the "stable" cultures around them, not against the people who gave birth to those local traditions. Emerson indulges in quoting one of Burke's self-defenses in making his case:

> "I am accused of being a man of aristocratic principles. If by aristocracy they mean the peers, I have no vulgar admiration nor any vulgar antipathy towards them; I hold their order in cold and decent respect. . . . If by the aristocracy . . . they mean an adherence to the rich and powerful against the poor and weak, this would indeed be a very extraordinary part. I have incurred the odium of

> gentlemen in this house by not paying sufficient regard to men of ample property. When indeed the smallest rights of the poorest people in the Kingdom are in question, I would set my face against any act of pride and power countenanced by the highest that are in it; and if it should come to the last extremity, and to a contest of blood, God forbid; God forbid, my part is taken—I would take my fate with the poor and low and feeble." (*EL* 1: 194)

While Burke continues to say that if the lowly seek an "exemption not from power but from the rules of morality" he would side with the latter, Emerson uses this lengthy quotation to highlight Burke's self-proclaimed position of defender of the common man.

This trait of defending the common man is the third that Emerson highlights and confers on Burke, and is, in Emerson's estimation, "a habitual ascendency" that helped him make associations between the "incongruous characters" of "a philosopher and a partisan" (*EL* 1: 196). By discerning greater order, by seeing within nascent democracies the voice of virtue, Burke reconciled not only his own worldview but those of his sparring partners in Parliament as well. He accomplished this, according to Emerson, by enacting a special kind of eloquence that only a few ever achieved.

Emerson's Cicero and Burke's "Philosophic Eloquence"

Emerson's fascination with eloquence is part of a broader "culture of eloquence" that has been widely discussed by both literary and rhetoric scholars, one that emerges in part from a fascination within the New Republic for Ciceronian eloquence. In the early nineteenth century, Cicero had come to represent a difficult problem in rhetoric. On the one hand, Cicero yoked together virtue and eloquence in a system that highlighted the positive change that a good orator could make in a society, but on the other hand, he insisted that only a lofty way of speaking could truly motivate an audience to contemplate and act on great ideas. In book 3 of *De oratore*, he enumerates three styles, and he associates a different mode of rhetoric for each. The plain style was simple, clear, and direct, and at its heart was a sense of perspicuity and decorum. The middle style was even, calm, even charming. An orator of this type uses some simple figures of speech, but maintains a type of reserved dignity that rises above the more informative plain-style speakers. The grand style (sometimes called the "lofty," "ornate," or "grandiloquent" style) was used by orators with the greatest command of the language. It could be highly ornate, even opulent, and it had within it the capacity to change hearts and move men to act in unexpected ways.

As Kenneth Cmiel so effectively argues in *Democratic Eloquence*, nineteenth-century America saw the emergence of a plain style that, for many commentators, embodied genuine eloquence despite its apparent rejection of the lofty style. For Cmiel, this "middling style" evaded the pomposity of Ciceronian lofty style in order to connect common, everyday speech to eloquent expression. While the middling style avoided "the vulgar," it nonetheless relied on common expressions and the language of the street to the degree that what might have once been inappropriate for public speaking became overvalued as a representation of genuine character and virtue. Cmiel argues that "cultivated and vulgar cultural categories still existed but the clear sociological correlations of earlier times eroded," such that successful speakers "mixed together high and low language to fit their needs. Their speech was at times refined but at other times crude. They were often eloquent but they were also often folksy" (12–14).

Cmiel sees this mixing as partly a reaction to the excesses of an overwrought, misappropriated Ciceronian lofty style. He notes that while Cicero's rhetoric had, in part, focused on forging relationships between different types of communities, his lofty style had been mistaken by subsequent generations as demonstrative of good character, clear thinking, and sophistication. American suspicion of aristocracy and what Cmiel calls the "aristocratic misuse of civil language" (49) reigned in the streets despite the fact that Cicero had imagined the highly figurative use of language as appropriate for common folk who needed to be swept along by their passions (35). Ornate language, therefore, was reserved for the common people who might simply stand in awe of sophisticated figures and metaphors, whereas a more direct language would be used with legislators because of their wisdom.

This distinction leads to, for Cmiel, remarkable favoring of simple and direct speech in America as well as profound suspicion of people speaking in lofty ways. The marriage of the two—the low and the high—became a central problem for the culture, and one remedy was romantic rhetoric, which "conjured up a democratic version of the sublime by merging the lofty with the rustic" (95). This remedy Cmiel names as a special kind of middling style: the humble style. The humble style attempts to bridge the gap by drawing distinctions along the lines of personal character. The vulgar word in the hands of a humble speaker becomes eloquent, even as the same speaker is able to lift audiences to new heights of contemplation. In this formulation, Cicero, whose lofty style betrayed an inherent distrust of the masses, gives way to the humble speaker, whose down-home, folksy words embody an inherent honesty and truthfulness that only the common folk can truly understand.

Emerson was enamored with this type of rhetoric, as it appealed to his sense that the humblest and simplest citizens could raise others to action and shape the course of a country. As early as spring 1833, before he had left his career in the pulpit, he expressed this sentiment at length in his journals:

> How well men know in what churches & individuals the religious principle is found. Yet we think we can convince men, by talking, that we are in the right. All the reasons in the world may be piled together, all the solemn words in the language may be repeated, yet if only the Understanding is addressed your cause is not won. But let a graceless and ignorant man arise who is now exercised by the religious sentiment[,] who follows after the beauty of holiness and he out of his heart will speak to yours. His words are loaded. They penetrate into the soul and will call up the deep & divine powers from their long sleep, and the awe-struck understanding shall now be still & docile. Let the laws of thought be stated, & people learn that master rule of Rhetoric, that things go by number & weight, and pass for what they be, not by seeming. (*JMN* 5: 144)

Associating powerful rhetoric with spiritual action is central to much of Emerson's work and will be explored further in the following chapter, but here, Emerson links that power to the common man who, though lacking formal training, nonetheless speaks with a masterful expression and force. The "graceless and ignorant" here becomes eloquent. As he would write elsewhere,

> the language of the street is strong. . . . Cut these words & they would bleed; they are vascular & alive; they walk & run. Moreover they who speak them have this elegancy, that they do not trip in their speech. It is a shower of bullets, whilst Cambridge men & Yale men correct themselves & begin again at every half

> sentence. . . . Yet always this profane swearing & bar-room wit has salt & fire in it. . . . *Guts* is a stronger word than intestines. (*JMN* 7: 374)[5]

The physicality of Emerson's description animates the passage. Drawing on visceral and violent images, he describes a language that overwhelms the halting words of the educated classes with its sheer power. The lowest class here becomes the most powerful.

Emerson, then, is keenly invested in what Cmiel calls the humble style, and his fascination with the "language of the street" explains why Cicero and Ciceronian eloquence figure largely in his corpus yet typically appear only in passing and with remarkably little extended discussion. Emerson often includes Cicero as one of his great minds, speakers, or writers, but when it comes to developing a full picture of Cicero, Emerson is strikingly quiet. Cmiel's analysis of the tension between Ciceronian lofty style, which aimed to deliver soul-shattering truths, and American humble style, which aimed to deliver straight-talking, down-home wisdom, elucidates why Emerson could not abandon the latter even while he adored the orientation toward divine principles of the former. He wanted to invoke Cicero's pining for spirit while endorsing a commoner's rhetoric.

By 1831 at the latest, Emerson had read from Cicero's complete works, which include *De inventione* and *De oratore*, and we know that Emerson's library included *De officiis*, along with four other works. These selections account for the main body of Cicero's thinking on rhetoric and suggest Emerson's engagement with Ciceronian rhetorical theory, but the Cicero who appears in Emerson's work is largely the American representation of Cicero, one that simultaneously extends rhetorical power to the common person even while it grants that the commoner can be duped by inflated styles. This highlights that for Emerson, Cicero was more of a trope, a figure to be invoked as a counter to his ongoing explorations of the individual's power within a democracy.

Almost a decade earlier in a letter to his intellectual and spiritual mentor Mary Moody Emerson, a young Emerson labels Burke "an improved Cicero" (*Letters* 7: 152). The contrast illustrates, on the one hand, Emerson's admiration for Burke's oratory and, on the other hand, Cicero's currency as a touchstone of oratory in early America. Cicero, in other words, already signified great eloquence, otherwise suggesting that Burke was superior would have been largely academic praise. When Emerson calls Burke "an improved Cicero," then, Emerson is suggesting that Burke moves beyond the ornamentation of Cicero-as-lofty-style representative in order to become the embodiment of what he later calls "man thinking." Instead of remaking Cicero into a humble speaker, he finds a better version of him for America. Edmund Burke is that example.

Emerson at times contrasts Burke with Cicero in his lecture on the former, especially when discussing eloquence, in order to highlight Burke's stature over Cicero. This maneuver illustrates that Emerson, still young in his lecturing career, was conversant with the cultural anxiety about the types of rhetoric circulating in antebellum America and was seeking a solution. Emerson recommends Burke as a model and argues that "he is a new and original person, in manner, act, and word, that he derived his inspiration from the facts themselves to which he spoke and not from vanity or selfish ends," a trait best articulated with the phrase that another speaker once quipped: "Burke did not resemble Tullius Cicero . . . he resembles Edmund Burke" (*EL* 1: 197). Burke's originality and sincerity make him stand alone, and comparing him to Cicero failed to capture his originality. In all, Burke, in specific moments in his career,

> did embody the idea of eloquence, when he did fill the ear and mind and heart of his hearers and produce the perfect triumph of the orator which consists in the oneness of his audience. . . . [and] soared above all the praise of Demosthenes or of any civil orator. (*EL* 1: 198–99)

Emerson's elevation of Burke above both Demosthenes and Cicero as practitioner of eloquence would have been extraordinary praise to level, at a time when Cicero was the most important model of eloquence for Americans.

Despite the high praise of Burke, however, Emerson's theory of rhetoric as outlined in "Edmund Burke" is itself an Americanized Ciceronian hierarchy. Like Cicero, Emerson wants to relegate true eloquence to a special sphere of discussion, but unlike the American imaginings of the more formal Cicero, he wants to grant wider access to that sphere. Accordingly, he finds in Burke a model for speaking plainly and directly and yet forcefully and eloquently. He labels Burke's special kind of eloquence "philosophic eloquence," declaring that "even now in the British and American Senates[,] Mr. Burke is the founder and head" of this particular school of speaking (*EL* 1: 200). This type he contrasts with two other forms of eloquence, and he spends the closing pages of the lecture describing the three forms. It would be the closest Emerson ever came to creating a taxonomy of rhetoric.[6]

The first form of eloquence, "Natural Eloquence," resides in "certain felicities of voice and manner." Those with natural eloquence speak largely "by heart" and "not by the mind," and while an audience "delights to hear" this type of speaker, "the hearer returns home intoxicated with excitement and venting himself in superlatives, [yet] he cannot recal [*sic*] a reason, a statement, scarce a sentiment even for the curiosity of inquirers." This type of speaker relies on pathos: "No arguments have been used, no ground of facts shown" (*EL* 1: 199).

The second form is "practical" eloquence, which "treats it [eloquence] as a question of business and contemptuously setting aside all sentiment and all general considerations as remote, exhibits one prudential aspect of the affair and neither enlightening nor obscuring, awakens no emotion but extorts votes" (*EL* 1: 199–200). In this mode, fact is all, and meaning, connection, and significance are left aside. The singular fact acts as a kind of tyrannical certainty whose only power is to "extort" action by insisting on its certainty.

The final type of eloquence Emerson calls "philosophic eloquence." To Emerson's mind, this was a kind of true eloquence in that it yoked mind and heart and brought together all the best features of natural and practical eloquence and reshaped them to give them meaning, purpose, and substance. While Emerson decries that most people "have more heart than mind," philosophic eloquence brings the two together, not so much as equal parts of a whole, but as a unified approach to securing an end. The nature of how they work together might best be called a concentration of power, whereby natural and practical eloquence provide raw material for the shaping of a final message, and in that process of shaping, the audience itself participates in an act of shared meaning-making. Eloquence, then, is more than simply persuasion by fact or by emotion, but is instead an elevation of speaker and audience to a shared (and perhaps necessary) truth.

Emerson places Burke in this final category, though he does so with significant qualification. He asserts that "only rarely does Mr. Burke rise to Eloquence." When he does, he is able to "concentrate attention upon the facts" while also considering "them in accordance with the immense expansion in modern times of all the powers of society" (*EL* 1: 200). In other words, facts, in his hands, transformed into broad power to connect diverse parts of the culture. Burke's words rose to the level of transformation, however, only "rarely," and Emerson indicates this deficit by labeling him a "Rhetorician":

> If the word Rhetoric had not by misuse acquired a hollow sound he might be called a consummate Rhetorician, being a sort of artist or painter with words and so fond himself of the exercise of this peculiar talent that he cannot deny himself the delight of adorning with his beautiful sketches every name and topic how flat and obscure soever that he touches.
>
> Grace is natural to him like genius of the Greeks . . . , so is he incapable of an inelegance. Whatever he touched he adorned. Whatever he has said can never be repeated with equal happiness. He will be the accepted formula for that sentiment. His naming a man is fame, for always the image of that man reappears in the dress Burke bestowed. (*EL* 1: 200–201)

Emerson's distinction here between eloquence and rhetoric is important because it reveals his refusal to make *rhetoric* synonymous with self-interest and deceit. Indeed, he links rhetoric with a natural capacity for grace, one with the remarkable power to forge itself as model for future speakers, but also the power to bestow fame through its "dressing" of a person or topic under discussion. Burke's moments of eloquence, then, come as part of his role as a rhetorician who, like an artist, paints only with beauty. Indeed for Emerson, Burke is, like all great artists, incapable of denying himself the impulse to paint—"to adorn"—his words.

This inability to turn away from adorning his speeches suggests how Emerson is able to connect Burke to philosophic eloquence, even if Burke is an imperfect example of it. Emerson celebrates throughout his career the ability of a true artist to make even the most mundane or quotidian aspects of life beautiful and significant. Emerson's fascination with Whitman's verse provides a ready example, as does his fascination with Emanuel Swedenborg. But just as Whitman and Swedenborg fall short of the ideal artist that Emerson imagines, Burke falls short of a life as the "true orator," even if he at times rises to embody it. This tension between philosophic eloquence and rhetoric helps Emerson explain Burke's political contradictions. Burke's support of American democracy is possible, for Emerson, because Burke saw in America no earlier traditions of "taste" that the new politics could upend, and so his "love [of] virtue . . . might well hesitate to decide between the continuance of tyranny and the outrageous abuses of freedom." As rhetorician, he saw in the

American political scene the beauty of new freedoms and new ways of governance, but as a figure of eloquence, he was unable to loosen his ties to the "ancient institutions, laws, nobility, priesthood, and crown." He was "unconsciously biased by his taste and imagination" (*EL* 1: 201).

The bias, however, does not reside in the process of "adornment." Burke's capacity to adorn his work with beauty instead points to his ability to connect with his audience, no matter how varied, and encourage them with what Stephen Browne has called a "discourse of virtue." Burke, Emerson asserts, "spoke to the world" (*EL* 1: 200), inveighing injustice against the poor and common and elevating the lowly in order to provide them with dignity and agency. His explicit condemnation of the prosecution of homosexuals, for example, got him labeled a sodomite. While his campaigns read today as paternalistic—wrapped in the language of aristocratic right and burden—and identify Burke as the father of those who have recently been described as the "moral-cultural guardians who were formulating a philosophy of responsible leadership by a natural aristocracy" (Maciag 4), they also point for Emerson to Burke's capacity to transcend class distinctions and persuade both noble and common to social action. Burke becomes, then, trope for a classless rhetoric, one that spoke to both high and low estates under the aegis of shedding "a little light in the dark and corrupt mazes of politics" (*EL* 1: 201). He acted with, as Emerson declares in his closing line of the lecture, "the devotion of a hero and the modesty of a child" (*EL* 1: 201).

This association—common man speaking forcefully, persuasively, and eloquently—allows Emerson to conflate the more learned domain of rhetoric and its attendant traditions and (at times) rigid methodologies, with eloquence, seen as organic, intuitive, natural. The lecture on Burke illustrates for the first time Emerson's repeated conflation of rhetoric, eloquence, and oratory, a habit he continues throughout his life even as he sometimes admits the more pejorative use of the term *rhetoric* in the culture of the time. It appears even in his later lectures, such as in "Celebration of Intellect," when he once again associates the common with both Burke and Cicero:

> But I value eloquence more when it is legitimate, when the talent is in true order, subject to genius, subject to the total and native sentiment of the man, and therefore in harmony with the public sentiment of mankind. Such is the patriotism of Demosthenes, of Patrick Henry, and of what was best in Cicero, and in Burke:

> not an ingenious special pleading, not the making a plausible case, but strong by the strength of the facts themselves. Then the orator is still one of the audience, persuaded by the same reasons which persuade them, not a ventriloquist, not a juggler, not a wire-puller paid to manage the lobby and caucus. (*LL* 2: 244)

Here, Emerson suggests that the orator is most powerful when he is "still one of the audience [members]" and invokes a shared knowledge, making it visible to them for the first time not by "special pleading" or trainings but by recourse to a native fact. Just as he traced out much earlier in the lecture of Burke, Emerson suggests eloquence is rhetoric, not because eloquence grudgingly admits vapid ornamentation of "mere rhetoric" into its domain, or because rhetoric subsumes eloquence as a special mode of expression, but because rhetoric, in the best sense, is sublime, even if it were plain. In other words, to speak rhetorically is to speak eloquently because rhetoric, as the natural expression of the common man, veered toward lofty ideals.

Emerson's near deification of Burke in this lecture puts the Irish nobleman on par with the greatest of orators. He embodies a rhetorical theory that, while democratic and justice-oriented, illuminated truth and drove audiences to right actions in the world. That Burke, as Drew Maciag argues in his examination of Burke's "contested career," is appropriated in so many different ways by American admirers and detractors speaks to the complexity of Burke's positions. Indeed, it highlights some of the very traits that Emerson found so valuable in Burke and others like him. It is unsurprising, then, that a later disciple of Emerson's, Franklin Sanborn, would in 1886 deliver a lecture in which he calls Cicero "the most illustrious Roman disciple of Plato," effectively rounding out a connection between Cicero, Plato, and Burke that Emerson would surely have endorsed (Ms Am 1746.1, p. 1).

3. RHETORIC, HERMENEUTICS, AND SUBMISSION

Emerson's Augustine and "the Art of Subliming a Private Soul"

Near the end of his 1867 lecture "The Preacher," Emerson asserts that "the essential ground of a new book or a new sermon is a new spirit" (*W* 10: 233).[1] The line is emblematic of Emerson's ongoing insistence that language owes its power to something beyond human agency, that the will and force of the writer or orator does not alone account for the power of language to enact social change. He would trace this idea through several essays and lectures, examining it from new angles and suggesting new paths for arriving at a similar conclusion even in some of his earliest speeches. That Emerson would, in 1879, deliver a version of this lecture at the Harvard Divinity School, where some forty years earlier he had called for a complete reenvisioning of the role of the divinity program so to emphasize the convertible power of the individual soul, speaks to the lecture's significance. It was Emerson's last official return to Harvard, the place where he had once directly challenged the formalism that he believed destroyed the heart of religious sentiment. In his 1838 "Divinity School Address," he called for a new vision of the preacher's power, one grounded in individual connection to divinity, and in 1879 he would deliver a similar message, this time stressing the necessity of spiritual resignation to divine will. It would be one of his last lectures, ending a career that began and ended with reflection on the role of the preacher in a culture. After it, he delivered only one more lecture, a final farewell to the Concord Lyceum in 1880.[2]

For Emerson, the preacher's special task is to help make the divine Word public, to help spirit move within a society. His frustration with what he called "historical Christianity" in the "Divinity School Address" certainly focused in part on the formal structures, rituals, and liturgies that usurped meaning from the act of worship, but at the heart of that concern with formalism, as it would appear again and again in his life, is its limiting effects on the preacher. It fosters distance between a preacher's own life and divine expression in the world. In other words, the reason that formalism in the church was so noxious was that it placed an intermediary—in this case rules and regulations—between an individual and his understanding of his place in the world. That place could only be understood in relation to what Emerson called the "beautiful necessity," the "oversoul," and various other names. Emerson's goal, then, was to shift the role of the preacher away from enforcer of liturgical correctness and church tradition and toward the role of mutual explorer for the nature of truth. That exploration, enacted through a cooperative moment of submission to divine insight, leads to a new vision of ethos, one that Emerson foregrounds in his rhetoric as he tries to articulate the relationship between audience and rhetor.

When the power to effect social change is assigned to divinity, the purpose of the rhetor shifts considerably. His role is no longer to seek out available means or persuasion or to devise a style adapted to the needs of an audience, but instead to resign himself to a greater power that can give his words force. He becomes a vehicle for divine expression that holds limitless power.

This submission to greater power marks a decided point of departure from many rhetorical theorists, and it remains an aspect of rhetoric that has received very little scholarly attention. While scholars in literature have long recognized a sense of resignation or submission in literary prose and poetics, rhetoric scholars, schooled in Aristotle's rhetoric and its heirs, have yet to fully account for a tradition that asks the rhetor to, on the one hand, speak powerfully, while, on the other hand, to assume such power only through an obliteration of the self.[3] Augustine is the centerpiece of this vision of rhetoric, and Emerson is his most obvious American heir.

Augustinian Rhetoric and a Hermeneutics of Resignation

Augustine outlines his theory of rhetoric in *De doctrina Christiana*, a work that was written over a period of thirty-one years, with the last book completed in 427 CE. The final book most explicitly traces Augustine's rhetorical theory, and it remains the work most frequently examined by scholars in rhetoric. As William Babcock points out, book 4 is "a manual for those who face the task of setting forth the truth of Scripture in clear and persuasive speech" (145), whereas the first three books represent "an attempt to delineate a system of significations that defines and sustains the culture of social order" and separates people as "lovers of eternal things or lovers of temporal things" (157). The previous three books, which can best be described as a theory of hermeneutics, are the foundation for the fourth book, and they suggest the primacy of the act of interpretation to any act of rhetoric. Hermeneutics is fundamental to rhetoric in this formulation, and for Augustine it provided a means by which the preacher subordinated himself to divine will.

Augustine's biblical hermeneutics assisted priests in unlocking the power of the Bible. The purpose was to provide them with insight into the Word of God, and his hermeneutics prepares them for eventually communicating the lessons of Scripture and biblical truth. Indeed, the priest must not renounce his obligation to speak because, as Philip Burton points out, "speech . . . is the characteristic activity of the Son of God, the Word who is intimately linked with the whole process of creation" (17). Once prepared through various interpretive stages, the priest employs a rhetoric that Augustine recommends in book 4. As John Cavadini points out, then, book 4 is "less a theory of rhetoric *per se* than a theory of conversion" (164). With an understanding of Scripture in hand, the priest who has engaged in the hermeneutic task of deciphering the Bible can move on to communicating the truths that have been revealed to him in order to change the heart of parishioners.

The hermeneutic Augustine establishes is a tiered method of interpretation that relies on the notion that the Bible is purposefully ambiguous and that its meaning is obscured to prevent casual readers from unlocking its mysteries. Augustine argues that the ability to understand the obscured Word of God comes only through constant study, prayer, and the elimination of the self in the act of interpretation. Indeed, the self must be utterly abandoned so that only the will of God guide interpretation: "Before all it is necessary that we be turned by the fear of God toward a recognition of His will, so that we may know what He commands that we desire and what He commands that we avoid" (*On Christian Doctrine* 38). Once turned to the will of God, the priest employs a hierarchized hermeneutic to resign himself to God so that he can be prepared by God to receive the multiple layers of the meaning in the Word. First, the reader must reflect on his mortality and future death. Second, the reader must become "meek through piety so that [he does] not contradict Divine Scripture" (38). Next, he must exercise acts of love that Augustine describes in book 1, among which are loving God for himself and loving one's neighbor for the sake of God. Once this love is in place, he must, in the fourth step, "extract himself from all mortal joy in transitory things, and . . . turn toward the love of eternal things," especially the Trinity (39). If he can truly absorb the meaning of the Trinity, he is then able to move to the fifth step, the counsel of mercy. This step helps him perfect the appropriate love of his neighbor for the sake of God, at which point he can rise to the sixth step, love of his enemy, a love that "cleanses the eye through which God may be seen." With God in full view, the reader can finally achieve the seventh step requisite for true interpretation of Scripture: peace and tranquility achieved by forgoing any desire to impress one's neighbor or do wrong to one's enemy (40). As the priest studies more regularly and consistently, and as he refines his prayer, he begins to see the message of God because he has obliterated his sense of self. In its place is a divine peace that grants the reader of Scripture access to the meaning of the obscured language of the Bible. Indeed, God manifests himself in the Word, so that the priest gains a kind of direct access to divine power once he has prostrated himself before the Word and become a vessel of God's love.

The key here is that understanding Scripture and employing its power come only through submission to God's will. Augustine insists throughout the first three books that only through a total resignation of individual will can an interpreter enter into the power of the text. For instance, at the closing of book 2, he maintains that only "when the reader has been prepared by this instruction so that he is not impeded by unknown signs, with a meek and humble heart, subjected easily to Christ with a burden that is light, established, rooted, and built up in charity so that knowledge cannot puff him up" will he be able to begin to examine the ambiguity of the Bible (78).

The hermeneutic act, then, occurs only through an act of abandonment. The self is left behind, and all human agency is cast off in order to allow the divine Word to flow freely from the text and grant the reader understanding of the ambiguities of Scripture. Indeed, more broadly, God uses the believer in order to spread Christ's message of charity, despite the ambiguities of human existence:

> For God loves us, and the Divine Scripture comments on His great love for us. How does He love us? So that He may use us, or so that He may enjoy us? If He enjoys us, He needs some good of ours, but no sane person would say this. For every good of ours either is God or comes from God. To whom is it obscure or doubtful that a light does not need the brightness of the thing it illuminates? For the prophet says most openly, "I have said to the Lord, thou art my God, for thou has no need of my goods." Therefore he does not enjoy us but uses us. For if He did neither, I cannot see how He could love us. (27)

God's use of the believer forms the foundation of Augustine's insistence that the believer abandon his own will to the will of God. Though Augustine is clear that God uses all of humanity, even if individuals have not submitted to him, it is those believers who have resigned totally and have taken up the act of understanding the Word of God that he most explicitly exhorts to find charity and from whom he imagines spiritual power to flow.

This act of a reader's resignation marks the most significant point of contact between the first three books and the fourth one of *De doctrina*. Augustine's return to the idea of resignation in book 4 suggests that the hermeneutic he outlines earlier must be a foundation for any theory of rhetoric. Augustine held firmly to the notion that submission to divine will was requisite for eloquent expression, and he carries the idea of resignation from hermeneutics to rhetoric. He prefigures this shift, expanded in book 4, in book 2 when he briefly discusses the "rules of eloquence": "Men did not themselves institute the fact that an expression of charity conciliates an audience, or the fact that it is easy to understand a brief and open account of events, or that the variety of a discourse keeps the auditors attentive and without fatigue" (71). Here, Augustine proposes that key elements of eloquence, like how to join with an audience and how to keep an audience interested, derive from divine plan, not from human invention. In book 4, he ensures that any reader of Scripture who in turn seeks to communicate truth understands that the power of eloquence is not his own, but God's.

Augustine argues that genuine persuasion is, in fact, a manifestation of divinity in the material world: "For these words were not devised by human industry, but were poured forth from the divine mind both wisely and eloquently, not in such a way that wisdom was directed toward eloquence, but in such a way that eloquence did not abandon wisdom" (132). For Augustine, the wisdom of eloquence, its moral propriety and rightness, does not emerge from the right usage of words, arrangement, or by its applicability to a particular situational context but by the divine pouring forth of truth.

Augustine's insistence that true Christian rhetoric be preceded by prayer on the rhetor's part indicates Augustine's initial move to shift rhetoric's power from the rhetor back to divine immanence. He exhorts the priest to pray before both the hermeneutic task of reading the Bible and before any preaching (140), invoking Matthew 10:19–20: "'Take no thought how or what to speak: for it shall be given you in that hour what to speak. For it is not you that speak, but the Spirit of your Father that speaketh in you'" (140). Augustine's choice of biblical quotation here suggests that in public speaking, human agency is not sufficient to carry the power of the Word; that, in fact, God animates the priest's rhetoric to change the heart of a parishioner. The ultimate result is that judgment about what constitutes eloquence rests not in the opinion of the audience but in the rhetor's adherence to the divine principles set forth by the Christian God in the Bible: "When he does this [teach what is good] well and properly, he can justly be called eloquent, even though he fails to win the assent of his audience" (142–43).

In Augustine's schema, rhetoric's persuasive action derives from its connection to transcendental truth, and its efficacy is judged not by audience reception but by obedience to transcendental principles. For Augustine, the Bible, in particular, is the source of these foundational judgments as to what is divinely eloquent, so that as a source and model of spiritual insight, the Bible becomes the exemplum of true eloquence.

To be clear, the manifestation of the Word in this configuration is not the spontaneous appearance of God in the world. Augustinian hermeneutics does not result in Calvinistic Great Awakenings. Instead, God becomes manifest in the words of the speaker through an act of submission to God's will in a process of discovery that gradually reveals the subtle and hidden meanings of the text. As Brenda Deen Schildgen points out, Augustine rejects "divinely inspired, unmediated insight" in favor of revelation through the difficult work of interpretation (383). Revelation, to hazard a paradox, requires profound work and study that is predicated on submission to a holy text. Hermeneutics manifests divine truth only to those readers who engage in a process of prayer, submission, and reading governed by the overarching principle of charity and love of God.

However, Augustine extends the power of the divine well beyond simply hermeneutics and, in doing so, crafts an entirely new understanding of rhetoric and persuasion. For Augustine, just as revelation occurs through interpretation, it may also occur in the act of expression. The speaker, simply by uttering words in his state of submission to the divine, may receive and communicate spiritual insights that might otherwise be reserved for the hermeneutic study of the Word. Indeed at times, revelation through expression occurs as an unintended consequence of the rhetor being immersed in the Word of God. In this formulation, the idea of purpose as central to rhetorical theory is entirely negated, as are other aspects of rhetorical delivery. Arrangement, audience consideration, word choice (all aspects of rhetorical craft and training) may vanish in a moment when the rhetor's will is obliterated in favor of the greater will rooted in divinity.

Augustine's assignation of the convertible power of rhetoric to God significantly shifts the role of the orator and preacher. His obsession early in book 4 with ensuring that the true orator be concerned first and foremost with wisdom (instead of eloquence) speaks to this shift. With wisdom at the root of expression, Augustine effectively argues that wisdom is in itself a type of eloquence, even if it is not always fully appreciated. Wisdom allows the orator to cast the burden of being eloquent onto divine power, trusting that God will convey truth persuasively through clarity and eloquence. The speaker grants the listener access to the divine truth not simply by explication of text but by "pronouncing it energetically" (*On Christian Doctrine* 132). The speaker is ultimately able to persuade

> more through the piety of his prayers than through the skill of his oratory, so that praying for himself and for those whom he is to address, he is a petitioner before he is a speaker. When the hour in which he is to speak approaches, before he begins to preach, he should raise his thirsty soul to God in order that he may give forth what he shall drink, or pour out what shall fill him. (140)

The orator, petitioning for grace and revelation, receives it and, in turn, shares it with his audience. In other words, oratorical study does not create the words to be shared; the orator receives them and passes them on for others to hear, understand, and even pronounce themselves "energetically."

This maneuver helps us better understand Augustine by explaining why in book 4's opening he so vigorously insists the he is not writing a handbook of rhetoric. Doing so would suggest that the art of rhetoric—of moving souls to God—derives simply from a set of rules and methods to be mastered. Instead, Augustine focuses on the primacy of the Bible as divine expression, and, in a radical rethinking of the capacity of the audience to discern truth, it allows him to explain how wickedness or evil cannot ultimately corrupt the communication of biblical truth. Even pagans or heretics can, in this formulation, communicate Christian truth.[4]

Augustine makes this case as he closes book 4. Mirroring the ideas he establishes in *The Teacher*, Augustine argues that even wicked men may speak truth because they are, on the one hand, vessels of God's will and, on the other hand, speaking God's divinely ordained Word. He argues that though a positive and virtuous ethos ultimately ensures the broadest dissemination of God's Word, "truth may be announced but not in truth, that is, evil and fallacious hearts may preach what is right and true." The result is that evil preachers "benefit many by preaching what they do not practice; but many more would be benefited if they were to do what they say" (164–65). That powerfully good persuasion can come from the lips of an evil or fallen preacher means that persuasion, at least in part, is not in the hands of the preacher. It is, instead, in the hands of God, who works through the priest regardless of his intent. Good words, especially Scripture, move people despite a rhetor's ethos.

While the job of Augustine's priest, then, is to study methods of delivery to ensure that he does not make obvious errors or misunderstand his role as a preacher, he has a greater obligation to immerse himself in the Word of God before he preaches. This alone leads to a change in character in order to guarantee that God has ultimate control over the act of persuasion. Accordingly, Augustine endorses Quintilian's "good man speaking well"; though in this instance, the goodness of the man derives from his intense study of Scripture even if Augustine claims that a speaker may, in fact, not be good and still communicate truth.

James J. Murphy's landmark discussion of Augustine should be seen in this light. Murphy argues that Augustine's mission was in large part to make rhetoric, a secular art of the fourth and fifth centuries, applicable and usable for the Christian priest. If that is the case, Augustine not only Christianizes rhetoric as a whole (as Murphy contends) but he also does so in part by subordinating the power of the priest to the power of the Word. He could only appropriate a pagan craft if, in fact, the underlying truth of that craft originates from a Christian God, no matter how obscured that derivation had become. Augustine spiritualizes rhetoric by first theorizing a hermeneutics of resignation that requires the rhetor to prostrate himself to the actual language he employs. In doing so, the speaker submits to a higher purpose. Augustine's rhetoric, largely a response to the Second Sophistic, contests the sophists' assignation of ultimate power to the speaker and reassigns it to the divine influence of a holy text. The preacher effectively hands over his power to a divine message that derives from the hermeneutic task of studying the Bible, and he resigns himself to the proposition that his word and life is secondary to God's plan to achieve genuine charity among his listeners.

Augustinian Resignation and Emersonian Submission

Several scholars have examined the ubiquity of a concept of resignation in Emerson's writing and thinking, though not directly in relation to his rhetoric. For example, Richard Poirier has written that Emerson's idea of self-reliance can only be understood as turning "recurrently to its opposite, to self-dissolution, to the abandonment of any already defined Self" (20). Christopher Newfield's influential *The Emerson Effect* similarly argues that for Emerson, "individualism comes to include submission" (6). Newfield links individualism with submission to a corporate will and traces a lineage of the linkage, calling it the "Emerson effect." He locates its influence across a tradition of American liberalism and, ultimately, economics. For Newfield, the resulting individualism can best be understood as "freedom as submission to unmodifiable law" (7), and he imagines "public, reciprocal, rule-making agency" of liberalism being replaced "by unity, by common principle, a higher law which is out of reach of the public sphere" (211).[5]

Newfield's assessment of Emerson focuses on the "public"-ness of this vision of submission. He suggests that Emerson's conflation of divine with public good moves his thinking from a type of Platonic essentialism to democratic antifoundationalism. While Newfield is careful to argue that Emerson never fully reconciles these worlds, his assessment remains problematic in that it never fully addresses Emerson's ongoing fascination with the idea of truth. Public, here, in other words, may not derive from a broad democratic view of what constitutes reality. Instead, it suggests that transcendental reality is by its very nature democratic and public. It is fundamentally accessible to all people. That accessibility, however, does not suggest a reality grounded in a plurality of meanings. In other words, just because Emerson figures the publicness of truth as a plurality of voices does not mean that the plurality is itself the truth. Instead, in works like "The Preacher," truth is the power to which all preachers must submit before their unique voices can evoke its reality in the minds of their auditors. It is, finally, the submission of the preacher that matters, not his individualized voice.

The importance of this sense of resignation to Emerson's theory of rhetoric is hard to overstate. It places Emerson squarely in a tradition that prioritizes the role of hermeneutics in the creation of powerful rhetoric, and it suggests that Emerson, like Augustine, envisioned rhetoric as something at least partially beyond the ability of the rhetor to master on his own. It suggests that rhetoric, at least in part, derives from something other than human agency.

Augustine's rhetoric provides a useful framework with which to understand how Newfield's "Emerson effect" plays out in Emerson's rhetorical theory. Emerson's appropriation of Augustine, however, originates not so much from direct homiletic study but from broader considerations of the relationship between self and divinity. Emerson's journals demonstrate his ongoing concern with how the self relates to some sense of deity, and they consistently invoke Augustine when considering that relationship.

Emerson positions Augustine as one of the "*Trismegisti*," which he defines as "that lofty and sequestered class who have been . . . [the intellect's] prophets and oracles." They are a "high-priesthood" who expound the "principles of thought from age to age." Along with Augustine, Emerson includes Jesus, Socrates, Confucius, Heraclitus, and Pythagoras (*JMN* 7: 37). Purportedly a descendant of Hermes himself, Hermes Trismegistus (from whose name Emerson's "*Trismegisti*" is taken) is the father of a certain vein of mysticism with roots in what came to be called hermeticism. Hermeticism held, among other doctrines, that one true faith governed the laws of the universe and could be found to be true within all religions. Trismegistus represented for Emerson an early example of a thinker who communicated universal truths through connection with the godhead. That Emerson associates Augustine with him is especially apt because for Augustine, Trismegistus represented a pagan mind capable of expressing Christian truth. Indeed, Augustine believed that he anticipated Christian faith. He exemplifies Augustine's centering of rhetoric's power on a universal and timeless God who communicates through speakers regardless of their particular religious orientation. If for Augustine, Trismegistus is the pagan speaking Christian truth, Augustine is for Emerson the doctrinaire speaking beyond the strictures of the church.

Augustine represents for Emerson a heroic voice that conjures the most powerful aspect of an age and can bring the reader to understand greater principles. He is capable of effecting powerful change and his work is worthy of a scholar's "idle time" because of its transformative, even mystical, power:

> We return to the house and Take up Plutarch or Augustin [*sic*] and read a page or two, and lo! the air swarms with life, the front of heaven is full of fiery shapes: secrets of magnanimity & grandeur invite us on every hand: Life is made up of them. Such is our debt to Literature. (*JMN* 7: 276)

Reading religious texts, here, invites visions of participation in the divine and underscores Emerson's belief in the transformative power of Augustine's word. More importantly, it suggests that revelation emerges from the act of reading.

Emerson was at times preoccupied with how reading required a kind of internal submission. In a telling example, shortly following the death of his son Waldo, he grapples with the relationship between reading, revelation, and living in the world, and he uses Augustine to try to make sense of that relationship. He copies a long passage from the *Confessions* into his notebook that focuses precisely on this point:

> "And being thereupon admonished to reflect upon myself I entered into the very inward parts of my soul by thy conduct & I was able to do it because now Thou wert become my helper. I entered & discerned with the eye of my soul (such as it was) even beyond my soul & mind itself the unchangeable light of our Lord. Not this vulgar light which is subject to the sense of flesh & blood nor is it as of the same kind. It was greater & as if it were much, & much more clear than the other, & as if it would possess the whole by the greatness thereof. This light I say was not that former light but another & very different from all these inferior things. Neither was it so above my understanding as oil swims above water or as the heaven is raised above the earth. But it is above me because it made me and I am under it because I was made by it." (*JMN* 6: 383)

The most remarkable quality of this passage is not its replication of the typical Emersonian desire to turn inward. Instead, the passage is noteworthy because it illustrates that Emerson's desire derives from "admonition" from a higher power. Further, it suggests that the clarity of perception comes not from the individual but from the higher power. Given Emerson's grief over the death of his son, the passage is probably not surprising. It proposes a remedy to his suffering by casting it as heavenly guidance. Nonetheless, it stands out as a passage that situates the movement to enlightenment within a framework of submission. It requires Emerson to abandon his own sense of development in favor of divine admonition and grace.

The sense that the self is absorbed into the greater currents of the universe emerges as a distinct influence on Emerson's conception of rhetoric and persuasion. In 1837, he encourages himself to set aside rhetorical tricks and feats of memory in order to let God direct his language: "But talk from the moment & do not shine but lie low in the Lord's power, wait & follow with endeavoring thoughts the incidents of the conversation, & you shall come away wiser than you went. You shall be uplifted into new perceptions" (*JMN* 5: 426–27). Similarly, reflecting on the relationship between extemporaneous speaking and silence, he declares that the former is as easy as the latter when a person is filled with emotion and "rises to his lips & overflows in speech": speaking requires that "he only adjusts himself to the free spirit which gladly utters itself through him. This is a practical lesson in the doctrine that there is but one Mind. Motion is as easy as rest" (*JMN* 5: 500).[6] For Emerson, just as for Augustine, the ultimate power to shape lives of auditors derives from a force other than rhetorical rules. Rhetorical power flows outward from God through the speaker to influence the minds and hearts of the listeners, and it is only by recognizing and resigning oneself to that power that the orator enacts true eloquence. Like Augustine, Emerson posits a hermeneutic that leads to submission to divinity as prerequisite to rhetorical acts. His hermeneutic, however, moves beyond holy Scripture to include a wider range of holy "texts" to be interpreted.

Emerson and "The Preacher"

Emerson's early homiletics have been well documented. Wesley Mott, in particular, has argued that Emerson's sermons demonstrate that he had for some time been grappling with romantic conceptions of the self and that his early journals depict a "searching young man whose self-conscious gropings toward eloquence are an intriguing prelude to the great Transcendentalist essays" (3). His early desire for eloquence in the sermon was paired with, according to Mott, an ongoing concern about the limitations of language in describing the religious experience; so that for Emerson, the act of interpretation and the act of preaching must paradoxically help the preacher approach and communicate the ineffable. Mott understands Emerson as seeing the purpose of oratory "as moral conversion with millennial stakes" (5), but that as his career advanced in the pulpit, "giving form to religious experience, describing and explaining the divine, presented no less a challenge to Emerson than to the Old Testament prophets, Catholic mystics, or his Puritan ancestors" (80). Mott notes Emerson's impatience with institutionalized expressions that attempt to express the divine, feeling that they can "entomb as well as express the felt experience of the Spirit" (80), and he suggests that Emerson would embrace the idea that the "the *experience* of God" is itself a "form of language" (95). Scripture, then, could be experienced, so that "reading the Bible critically enabled Emerson to connect revelation to voice and character" (95). All of this leads to the conclusion that Emerson's sermons prefigure his later romanticism, with its attendant aphoristic style in which "discursive logic is superseded by metaphorical brilliance and aphoristic pronouncements" (108). This style has been widely remarked on as indicative of Emerson's frustration with language that attempts to convince listeners and readers of truth as opposed to leading them to revelation of that Truth.[7]

If Mott's work establishes Emerson's early focus on how reading Scripture and preaching elicit revelatory experiences, it also illustrates Emerson's early attempts to negotiate how preachers and orators must submit themselves to a type of expression that escapes empirical demonstration of truth. As he writes in 1825, "eloquence is best inspired by an Infinite Cause" (*JMN* 2: 47). These early attempts become more pronounced as he grapples throughout his career with his own vocation as a sometimes frustrated orator. As Christopher Newfield's work suggests, the force with which the idea of submission controls Emerson's thinking becomes more pronounced as he ages. While Emerson's early statements on the role of preaching have received significant attention, his later declarations on the power of the preacher, which reflect a growing fascination with the idea of submission of the self to divine will, have received remarkably little. The later statements embody the idea of abandonment and resignation, and they reflect a decidedly Augustinian bent to his understanding of how language prompts social action.

In "The Preacher," one of Emerson's later lectures, he exhorts the preacher to effect social change through submission to a higher purpose.

Emerson insists throughout the lecture that most preachers have failed to reconcile new epistemologies (such as science) with old forms of religion, and the result is a stagnant faith that does little to uplift a congregation and, indeed, a whole society. In one version of the lecture, Emerson invokes Augustine as a member of the "real church" because, despite the deficiencies of Catholicism, the church answered God's call of the time (AC85.Em345.880p). The preacher now, however, stands at a crossroads in what Emerson calls a "moment of transition" (*W* 10: 217), and, in typical Emersonian form, he at once condemns contemporary preaching modes as deficient while simultaneously asserting the remarkable power available to pastors and parishioners alike. This power comes, ultimately, through submission to a universal force during acts of interpretation.

Emerson opens his lecture with a discussion of this moment of transition. Reflecting on the impact of science and industrial progress on faith and society, he sees a profound shift underway in America. While throughout the lecture he is at pains to embrace scientific progress, he nonetheless insists on a basic dualism that separates faith from science, religion from materialism. The result is that he finds "insight and truthfulness" among faith communities, but he cannot find "the gracious motions of the soul,—piety, adoration":

> Scorn of hypocrisy, pride of personal character, elegance of taste and of manners and pursuit, a boundless ambition of the intellect, willingness to sacrifice personal interests for the integrity of the character,—all these they have; but that religious submission and abandonment which give man a new element and being, and make him sublime,—it is not in churches, it is not in houses. I see movement, I hear aspirations, but I see not how the great God prepares to satisfy the heart in the new order of things. (*W* 10: 218)

Emerson's rhetorical maneuvering here highlights his admiration for certain elements of the rising materialism that has overtaken the church. His praise of a church informed by "ambition of the intellect" and personal sacrifice, however, is muted by his concern that a more sublime spirit has failed to run through it, and thus left it, as he argues in "Books," "dry on this side." The only remedy, he argues, is the way of resignation.

As "The Preacher" develops, Emerson increasingly demands a transformation of the pulpit to encourage abandonment to higher power. Throughout the opening pages of the essay, he confronts the problematic scientific epistemologies that have made their way into the pulpit, ultimately declaring that while they are "inevitable and useful," they are "ghastly in this empiricism" (*W* 10: 220). He uses the trope of battle to describe the result of the intellect dissecting the world without simultaneously seeking spiritual meaning: "When the game is run down, when the enemy lies cold in his blood at our feet, we are alarmed at our solitude; we would gladly recall the life that so offended us; the face seems no longer that of an enemy" (*W* 10: 220). The violence of the imagery suggests the barbarity of science in unraveling the mysteries of nature, but Emerson recognizes the inevitable impact of the field on the pulpit; so importantly, he does not simplistically attack the science as a method of inquiry and learning. Instead, he condemns certain uses of science, uses that seek "details" instead of "knowledge of the design" (*W* 10: 224). The true preacher, then, uses the findings of scientific progress as metaphors to be interpreted. He reads the natural sciences as a method to understand spirit. The preacher's hermeneutic task, then, is deciphering the meaning of scientific findings without losing sight of his dependence on universal power:

> All that we call religion, all that saints and churches and Bibles from the beginning of the world have aimed at, is to suppress this impertinent surface-action, and animate man to central and entire action. The human race are afflicted with St. Vitus's dance; their fingers and toes, their members, their senses, their talents; are superfluously active, while the torpid heart gives no oracle. When that wakes, it will revolutionize the world. Let that speak, and all these rebels will fly to their loyalty. (*W* 10: 224)

The "surface-action" here is a metaphor for the materialism that has moved America away from understanding divine law. To regain a center and thus act in the world in a meaningful way, humanity must cease its own attempts to act in favor of letting the oracle speak. That oracle creates a new kind of action, one that is tantamount to revolution and one that will move America from an age of transition to an age of ascendance.

Positioning the oracle as the path to true action establishes a difficult dichotomy for Emerson to reconcile. On the one hand, Emerson wants to assert the power of American progress. He wants to embrace the discoveries of the natural sciences, and he wants to trumpet the innovations of an industrialized state. On the other hand, Emerson wants those changes to be seen as a sign of spiritual power. He wants the preacher to read the American scene as a kind of biblical phrase that needs elucidation. Without that act of interpretation, the preacher becomes nothing more than a sensationalist "gazette" (*W* 10: 231). With a spiritualized hermeneutics, however, "inspiration will have advance, affirmation, the forward foot, the ascending state" (*W* 10: 233).

Thus equipped, the preacher turns inward and learns that his role is a grand affirmation of a profound spiritual power. That central power simplifies the purpose of the preacher to the celebration of revelation:

> The inevitable course of remark for us, when we meet each other for meditation on life and duty, is not so much the enjoining of this or that cure or burning out of our errors of practice, as simply the celebration of the power and beneficence amid which and by which we live, not critical, but affirmative. (*W* 10: 235)

The affirmative power here overwhelms any fixation on daily problems or even daily rumination on the particulars of faith. The preacher instead focuses on a "beam out of eternity," so that he might "retire a moment to the grand secret we carry in our bosom, of inspiration from heaven" (*W* 10: 236). This is the same power that Emerson extends to all people in other lectures, such as in "Table Talk," where he insists that "speech is power,—Speech is to persuade, to convert, to compel. It is to bring another out of his bad sense into your good sense. You are to be missionary of all that is good and noble" (*LL* 2: 363). The yoking of power to the "good and noble" here reflects the same mission of the preacher, whose purpose, "to convert," runs alongside persuasion to good sense.

Inspiration, revelation, and the ultimate turning of an audience's mind to a realization of the divine currents of the universe mean, for Emerson, that the preacher, while at once aware of the daily circumstances of his parishioners, also asks them to transcend those circumstances. This is not, however, simply repudiation of the world. Emerson embraces the progress and development of the industrialized state. What he desires, however, is that those advances take on metaphorical value to be interpreted and communicated. They become a text for the preacher to read within a spiritual framework. The preacher's work, then, is elucidation. It is the hermeneutic illumination of an otherwise meaningless sense of progress. Emerson, therefore, closes the lecture with the idea that the preacher interprets the world in a new way. He provides new angles of vision:[8]

> And when we go alone, or come into the house of thought and worship, we come with purpose to be disabused of appearances, to see realities, the great lines of our destiny, to see that life has no caprice or fortune, is no hopping squib, but a growth after immutable laws under beneficent influences the most immense. . . . We come to educate, come to isolate, to be abstractionists; in fine, to open the upper eyes to the deep mystery of cause and effect, to know that though ministers of justice and power fail, Justice and Power fail never. The open secret of the world is the art of subliming a private soul with inspirations from the great and public and divine Soul from which we live. (*W* 10: 237–38)

Emerson draws here on a long-standing Platonic duality, and his invocation of "upper eyes" contrasts the condemnation of "lower eyes" that see only "surfaces and effects" (237). Central to this split, however, is the idea that the upper eyes see more broadly, and they provide perception into a reality that governs all existence. Emerson asks the preacher and the parishioners here to submit to that higher reality, to open the upper eyes to the truth that, in the words of his journals, "the best part, I repeat, of every mind is not that which he knows, but that which hovers in gleams[,] suggestions[,] tantalizing unpossessed before him. . . . [T]hat vast revolutions, migrations, & gyres on gyres in the celestial societies invite him" (*JMN* 9: 341). The preacher must become "a live coal to kindle all the church" (*JMN* 5: 197). This invitation is the preacher's highest duty. Emerson exhorts the preacher to inspire the deep turn inward in order to encourage the recognition that insight comes from "subliming a private soul" and submission to the "great and public and divine Soul from which we live." If Augustine, as James J. Murphy argues, was making rhetoric a legitimate method of preaching for Christian orators, Emerson was encouraging preachers to embrace new visions of the self in deploying their particular forms of rhetoric. That vision requires resignation to divine will, which comes after a new reading of signs of divine immanence in the natural world.

Emerson had, of course, theorized this position long before his work on "The Preacher." *Nature*, as Alan Hodder has argued, might be seen as enacting this very kind of rhetoric, but Emerson continues this line of thinking throughout his career. For Emerson, the proverbial book of nature simply needed translation to makes its mysteries available to audiences. In 1840, he finds in nature the roots of rhetoric itself:

> There are two ways of speaking—One, when a man makes his discourse plausible & round by considering how it sounds to him who hears it, and the other mode when his heart loves & so infuses grace into all that drops from him. Only this is living beauty. Nature also must teach thee rhetoric. She can teach thee not only to speak truth, but to speak it truly. Only poets advance with every word. In most compositions, there is one thought which was spontaneous, & many which were added & abutted; but, in the true, God writes every word. (*JMN* 7: 386)

Emerson, here, juxtaposes an audience-based rhetoric with a resignation-based rhetoric. While one mode of speaking provides "plausible" expression, the other, which links truth to nature, originates from God. Indeed, God writes that language, and the speaker need only allow the spontaneous expression to "drop from him." Just as Augustine found perfect rhetoric in Scripture, Emerson finds perfect rhetoric in the book of nature.

Sandra Gustafson sees this sense of resignation in the Puritans. Writing about the development of rhetoric in the eighteenth century, she argues that "Puritan rhetorical theory sought to define forms of eloquence that did not in and of themselves persuade the audience. Only the Spirit could truly convert a saint" (33). Gustafson later notes that this idea that an individual does not create his or her own eloquence but merely functions as a vessel for God's eloquence has significant roots in the story of Paul. She points out that Paul renounced his own capacity for eloquence by insisting that God was responsible for making him persuasive, not his own will or his own method of study (274). The point here is that the tradition of resignation to divine will as the fount of eloquence is neither new nor unique to American rhetoric, but Emerson found useful precedence for this line of thinking in Augustine and (if Gustafson is right) some of the Puritan fathers. The religiosity of both, of course, bothered Emerson, so his dilemma was reconciling a belief in the need for submission to something holy and a desire to break from the liturgical features of church that he believed limited the genuine expression of God. Not finding that means of reconciliation in the church, he turned instead to nature, and there, as he discusses in "The Preacher," he found a text not only requiring interpretation but immutable laws governing the universe as well.

4. "*HABIT* OF HEAT"

Emerson, Belletristic Rhetoric, and the Primacy of the Imagination

In a manuscript folder containing Emerson's 1867 "Eloquence" lecture notes, his words are clear: "heat, heat" and "higher temperature" are necessary for eloquence. Emerson declares that the "history of Liberty will be the history of eloquence; as the Andes, Alleganies [*sic*] indicate the line of the fissure in the crust of the earth along which they were lifted Eloquence knows the line of caloric." The last few words, "Eloquence knows the line of caloric," are written with a different ink, a burning addition to the previous geological metaphor.

Emerson uses the metaphor of heat throughout his writings to describe the power of eloquence, and as he crafted a theory of rhetoric, images of fire, flames, and electricity come to dominate his vision of rhetoric's impact in the world. Rhetoric burned into souls, it opened fissures in the ground, and it charged the atmosphere with electricity. Emerson's repeated use of this imagery suggests that he believed rhetoric and eloquence had the power to disrupt the status quo, yet more than that, it speaks to his conception of rhetoric as something that is at times uncontainable, something grand and life-altering. The imagery contends that eloquence is anything but staid and refined; it is instead like a volcano, building beneath the surface until it explodes into the world at some unexpected moment.

Emerson conceived of rhetoric as having the power to change the world, to break apart dogma and reform civilization; and his vision of rhetoric helps clarify how nineteenth-century America attempted to negotiate the terrain between a rising romanticism, with its attendant focus on individual power, and the birth of a new nation, with a focus on responsibilities to and sense of duty required by the American state.

Emerson endeavored to connect the two, partially through rereadings of historical figures such as Plato and Burke, but also through forging connections between some of the central tenets of romanticism and some of the central ideals necessary to sustain a vision of democratic progress. Emerson sees rhetoric as a method by which to reconcile these competing demands, and in order to find that reconciliation, he links the imagination with social action, romanticism with civic duty. Drawing on figures like Hugh Blair and Dugald Stewart, even while rejecting American appropriations of those very same figures, Emerson posits rhetoric as an imaginative act that prompts popular action. He rejects a romanticism that is entirely divorced from civic duty while romanticizing rhetoric by prioritizing the role of the imagination in it. Emerson's conception of rhetoric is revolutionary in nineteenth-century America because it weds these two possibilities through emphasizing the imagination. Indeed, for Emerson, the imagination is not simply a central idea; it is the single most important quality of rhetoric because it, ultimately, generates the heat that creates the flames of social action. As he would say in one of his later lectures, "what a power: when combined with the analyzing understanding, Imagination makes Eloquence,—the art of compelling belief, the art of making people's hearts dance to his pipe, and carrying war and peace in either hand" (*LL* 2: 295).

Emerson and Literary Romanticism

Emerson's language theory has most often been read in terms of literary aesthetics and is usually seen as a romantic renunciation of Lockean philosophy.[1] Philip Gura, for example, has argued that Emerson is part of a tradition in the early nineteenth century that sought to reconnect language with nature and, with this connection, grant language meaning and power beyond sensory experience. In this tradition, emerging in part from early American theological debates and the theories of Emanuel Swedenborg and Sampson Reed, language might "originate in the intuitive experience available to all men" (9). Emerson's participation in this tradition leads Gura to argue that "nature yielded a vocabulary that explained man's relationship to the spiritual realm" (94).[2] In short, Emerson's linking of theological debates with considerations of the power of language and literature led him to grant language spiritual significance.

Emerson's exploration of language's relationship with nature and divinity, however, has implications beyond the creation of a literary aesthetic.

Emerson's rhetoric rests on some of the same foundations that Gura uncovers in Emerson's language theory and aesthetic. James Warren has argued that some of these foundations emerge from Emerson's work on eloquence, but while Gura focuses on the theological language that gave rise to Emerson's theory, Warren offers a heritage of philosophical language (29–51). Warren focuses on the nineteenth-century debates surrounding the search for an Adamic language, and he argues that both Jacob Boehme and Charles Kraitsir had significant impact on transcendentalist conceptions of eloquence. Most importantly, Warren identifies Emerson's reformist bent as deriving from some of those early theorists, leading him to associate the impulse to reform with a social theory of eloquence. According to Warren, "the reform of that most institutionalized of institutions—language itself—will lead, Emerson suggests, to the reform of the theological, educational, and literary institutions that employ language to constitute the culture at large" (47). Central to this reformation is a conception of language as action, so that for Emerson, "eloquence redraws conventional boundaries between contemplation and action" (47). In this figuring of Emerson and his language theory, the romantic ideal of spiritual contemplation is yoked inextricably to social action, and it suggests that understandings of Emerson as romantic philosopher or poet divorced from the concerns of culture ignore Emerson's regular attempts to redraw a romantic language theory based on the power of eloquence. This new romanticism prioritizes the role of the imagination in the communication of higher principles and reflects Emerson's ongoing study of how language grants access to divine principles through nature without recourse to theological doctrine. In addition, it weds a spiritualized language theory with social action.

Gura, Warren, and others who have articulated various versions of Emerson's thoughts on language ultimately situate Emerson in very specific cultural and philosophical contexts; indeed, Gura is careful to note that his work does "not claim to treat his [Emerson's] *overall* aesthetic theory with any degree of completeness" and that his focus is primarily on "what he [Emerson] did with the theological language and symbols he inherited" (180). These studies, which focus on philosophical and theological contexts, provide instructive ways of reading Emerson's conception of language. They also, however, run in many instances parallel to a rhetorical tradition that was emerging forcefully in the early part of the nineteenth century. As historians of rhetoric have demonstrated, the rhetorical tradition offered its own vision of the interaction between language and social action, and it emerges from and participates in many of the same philosophical and theological contexts that Gura and Warren explore.

Emerson's Surrounding Rhetorical Culture

Emerson was widely conversant with rhetorical culture of nineteenth-century America. Robert Richardson notes Emerson's sustained interest in eloquence and oratory throughout his career (the result of his study of rhetoric), and indicates that by late 1824, "he was working on 'eloquence' by reading every day in Cicero or Edward Everett," two rhetorical giants in Emerson's mind (58). At Harvard, Emerson was educated in belletristic rhetoric and captured a prize in declamation, modeling himself on his rhetorical idols. By the time Emerson was lecturing full time, he had read Plato's *Phaedrus* and the topic of "Eloquence" became among his most popular on the lecture circuit, one "as basic to Emerson as poetry" (R. Richardson 346, 447). Herbert Wilchens asserts that "at no time did he [Emerson] doubt that his task in life was to practice eloquence" (502), and both Roberta K. Ray and James Berlin note that Emerson lamented never having been offered a professorship in rhetoric, indicating that he had desired one "at Cambridge" (Ray 215; Berlin 42). This scholarship illustrates an Emerson who embraced the study of rhetoric, and it highlights Emerson's enduring concern for the power of eloquence throughout his career. The scholarship that seeks theological or philosophical roots for Emerson's thoughts on eloquence, then, while surely fruitful, has often neglected Emerson's own rhetorical context and thus some of the most compelling sources for understanding Emerson's combining of language and action.

During Emerson's lifetime, two major shifts occur in the history of rhetoric in New England educational culture. First, American eloquence flowers into the golden age of American oratory, with the lyceum and Chautauqua movements being established as popular arenas for the dissemination of knowledge, particularly in the sciences and new technologies. Second, as the nineteenth-century progresses, the term *rhetoric* increasingly becomes associated with the systematic study of written composition, so that by the 1880s, many textbooks on rhetoric are concerned solely with composition, not oratory. From the opening of the nineteenth century until the close, the study of rhetoric expands its realm of influence as professorships in rhetoric are established at a variety of colleges, including Harvard in 1806, and as the first courses dedicated solely to the study of college composition are established, also at Harvard, but not until the 1880s.[3] In all, the so-called American Renaissance embodies what Warren has called the "culture of eloquence," and F. O. Matthiessen, in his still useful assessment of the period, notes that Emerson recognized that eloquence was the one domain in which America had already formed a "literary tradition" (18).

Emerson, in short, was thoroughly steeped in a culture that valued the role of rhetoric in the formation of a democratic nation, and this culture had a rich heritage not only in philosophical and theological debates about the nature and source of language but equally in a history of rhetoric that pervaded American educational culture as well. This history of rhetoric maintained its own standards of propriety and expression, standards often enforced, sometimes implicitly, in the lyceum. These standards were quite distinct from those of theological and philosophical dialogue, and while there was surely interaction between the various disciplinary domains (particularly in the nineteenth century, when academic disciplines as we know them now simply did not exist), distinct traditions persisted in which students of rhetoric were educated. Emerson effectively bridges the gap between these worlds, theorizing and embodying a new ideal of American orator. This new ideal American orator is a radical departure from the orator and rhetorical writer proposed by most nineteenth-century American education, bringing to rhetoric the romanticism of his forebears and contributing to literature the need for social action.

The Rise of American Belletrism

While instruction in rhetoric became increasingly varied throughout the nineteenth century, even while it drifted toward a systemization of the rules of rhetoric, early and midcentury America was dominated by the New Rhetorics of the Scottish Common Sense School. The New Rhetorics of the eighteenth century emerged in large part from the work of George Campbell, whose *Philosophy of Rhetoric* embodies a "new" rhetoric in the rhetorical tradition because it attempts to bridge philosophy, rhetoric, and literature through the study of the science of the human mind. For Campbell and the New Rhetoricians, rhetoric and literature were linked in their sustained didactic purpose to educate and civilize the human mind. Rhetorical rules could be applied to all means of communication, and the way to access those rules was the systematic study of mental faculties. The faculties exhibited general properties that could be explicated and then generalized to rules for expression. As rhetorics established rules, then, they became increasingly linked to logic and rational discourse that both tames the natural instincts and directs the passions to proper expression. This taming of the passions, and, by association, of the imagination, translates to the increasing systemization of rhetoric, especially in American belletrism.

American belletrism borrows the New Rhetorics' fascination with the science of the human mind and applies it more broadly to the whole of belles lettres; however, American belletrism as a rhetorical movement descended most directly not from Campbell but from Hugh Blair's influential *Lectures on Rhetoric and Belles Lettres*. Blair's work was imported into New England colleges in the eighteenth century and remained the dominant text in rhetoric throughout the early nineteenth century. Blair's work was widely used by the schools as a way to mediate classical curricula, with its division between rhetoric, logic, and grammar, and, as Terence Martin indicates, it had been adopted by both Harvard and Yale by the late eighteenth century, shortly after its first publication. By the 1870s, Blair's work was essentially synonymous with rhetoric, and variations of it became the centerpiece of most composition courses when they first arose at Harvard.

Following Campbell, Blair recapitulates the New Rhetorics' gathering together of all means of communication and their reliance on reason and the rational discovery of the means of persuasion; and while he sees a significant part that the imagination might play, he subordinates it to reason and concerns of "taste," a New Rhetorical keyword that ensures that a moral prerogative drives all language use. For Blair, "the study of composition" is synonymous with "cultivating reason itself" so that "true rhetoric and sound logic are very nearly allied" (5–6). Imagination "serves reason in a special way because it allows the mind to apprehend aspects of truth . . . that cannot be directly perceived by the understanding" (N. Johnson, *Nineteenth-Century Rhetoric* 36). Even so, Blair insists that the imagination be governed by reason in order that taste be properly maintained. As part of the process of invention, therefore, imagination might be employed to determine a reasonable figure of speech to use in a given situation: "Figures, in general, may be described to be that Language, which is prompted either by the imagination, or by the passions" (Blair 146). The imaginative faculty generates figurative tropes naturally (even the most vulgar person, according to Blair, can spin out metaphors [145–46]),[4] but those tropes must be reined in by reason: "As Language makes gradual process towards refinement, almost every object comes to have a proper name given to it, and Perspicuity and Precision are more studied" (150). Equally important, the belletristic concern with taste could be exercised through an imaginative modeling of tasteful writing. Blair's system prioritizes the use of *imitatio* as a way of learning the eloquence of master composers, so students cultivate taste through the imagination by building their work on foundational orators such as Cicero. Through imitation and the subordination of the passions to a rational process of invention, imagination becomes embedded in a broader concern with reason and a system of rules for eloquence.

Blair's focus on a system of rhetoric that valued reason, imitation, and propriety in language fit well with the newly introduced German model of higher education in America. The German design valued specialization and well-defined areas of knowledge, and it transformed Blair's rhetoric in America into a tightly regulated system of expression associated almost exclusively with controlled, proper language, grammar, and practicality, often completely ignoring any discussion of the imaginative powers of the mind. However, as Linda Ferreira-Buckley and S. Michael Halloran point out in their discussion of the publication history of Blair's *Lectures*, the way that Blair was received in America is still under consideration and is widely varied. Ferreira-Buckley and Halloran argue that though Blair's impact on American rhetoric is clearly profound, as evidenced by the numerous imitators in the American educational landscape, creating definitive conclusions about those imitators may be in large part premature (xviii–xix).

Nonetheless, numerous early nineteenth-century American theorists of rhetoric, drawing on Blair, highlight a rhetorical system focused on reason and practicality. For example, Edward T. Channing, who taught rhetoric to both Emerson and Thoreau, contends in his lectures that rhetoric is preeminently a practical craft, and he makes his claims from a background that, as Terence Martin indicates, "strongly favored Common Sense philosophy at that time" (33). Channing should be seen as heir to John Quincy Adams, who, acting as Harvard's first Boylston Professor of Rhetoric and Oratory, argues in his *Lectures on Rhetoric and Oratory* (delivered between 1806 and 1809) that rhetoric is primarily a science that comes from a deeper moral sense capable of inspiring the imagination. Adams, and later Channing, however, is careful to stipulate that the imaginative faculty is too easily tempted to distortion, so that the rules of rhetoric, while not rhetoric itself, are in place to help control unfit uses of eloquence.

This need for rules to control the imagination is in keeping with belletrism's insistence that expression be regulated against moral collapse, so Channing, following Adams, is careful to schematize rhetoric in a way reminiscent of Blair and other Scottish rhetoricians. Martin, citing William Charvat, indicates that Channing is a central figure in the importation of not only the Common Sense philosophy but also Blair into American rhetoric instruction (15). The Blair influence is most pronounced in Channing's claim that "[rhetoric] seems to be strictly an instrumental art. It creates nothing, and, in one sense, bestows nothing. . . . Its work is, guidance, direction, and farther development . . . in a word, to bring into system the natural practice of all men" (41–42). This bringing "into system" requires most simply the articulation of universal truths about expression and language, so that to create a system of expression is to recognize and organize the most universal traits of rhetoric. As Channing develops the role of this system throughout his lectures, he demonstrates primarily that these universal traits lead to a clear sense of taste. For Channing, both the speaker and the listener in the rhetorical act are bound by the rules of taste. This systemization, in typical belletristic fashion, helps to control the imagination from firing the human passions too strongly, so that "the most sincere passion needs the restraint of taste, and the moderation, the serenity of self-possession" (59).

Adams and Channing, as lecturers at Harvard, illustrate the influence of belletristic rhetoric on the New England educational scene, but the breadth of the Scottish influence can perhaps best be seen in antebellum textbooks on rhetoric. Samuel Newman, in a widely circulated American book on rhetoric in antebellum America, provides one of the most far-reaching systems modeled after Blair and Richard Whately and stands as an emblem for the culture against which Emerson would make his arguments. Even though Newman's work self-consciously attempts to address the problem of "imagination," his *Practical System of Rhetoric* (1830) is caught between the world of an Americanized Blair and the world of imaginative discourse. On the one hand, he wants to correct what he sees as Blair's error of omission, but on the other hand, he attempts to provide a "practical" rhetoric.

Newman, as antithesis to Emerson, positions imagination as subordinate to a rational discovery of the means of persuasion, but he recognizes the strictures of the contemporary rationalist modes. He writes in his manual for writing instruction that "in our courses of study, we have discipline for the memory, for the reasoning powers in their various forms, and for invention. But no regard is paid to the exercise and improvement of the imagination" (vi). Despite Newman's desire to address the lack of exercise of the imagination and his desire that his students "become conscious of their own powers of imagination" (vii), his manual nonetheless participates in the same New Rhetorical tendencies it desires to circumvent. Newman begins his work with a response to the "complaint" that "the study of Rhetoric is of little practical advantage," conceding that there is merit to the complaint but that his system is both practical and uniquely adapted to American culture (1). The structure of the work highlights this practicality and desire for systemization, as does the way in which Newman addresses such topics as invention and literary taste and criticism. Beth Hewett's assertion that Newman drew from Whately's work in his revisions and new editions demonstrates the degree to which rhetoric was becoming linked to rational, scientific, and practical crafts because it is Whately who assigns rhetoric as a branch of logic. Its form, ultimately, is that of a practical handbook, its organization modeled after Blair. Emerson overturns this form and makes the form part of the content of an imaginative rhetoric.

Emerson's Challenge to Belletrism and Common Sense Rhetorics

In conceiving of an imaginative form of rhetoric, Emerson explicitly repudiates the formalism of American belletristic rhetorics like Newman's. He insists "that a whole Scotland of argumentation does not really help us" (*LL* 1: 150). Closely paralleling his break from Unitarian theology and its formalism, he signals a departure from American belletrist rhetoricians' appropriations of Blair, but just as his break from Unitarianism presupposed an early participation in it, Emerson's early career in rhetoric is absorbed in the belletrist school. Emerson studied Blair at Harvard, and Sheldon W. Liebman demonstrates how his early admiration for Blair led to a focus on perspicuity, ornament, and rational and controlled language use in his writings at Harvard, including his Bowdoin Prize essay in 1821 (181). Liebman points out that Emerson even showed a desire to write an essay on the evils of imagination (183). Nonetheless, by the time he delivered "The American Scholar" in 1837, he had declared his dissatisfaction with belletristic rhetoric on the grounds that it stifled the imaginative impulse. In this address, as will be seen, he decries the formality of belletristic education, echoing his 1837 lecture on "The Present Age," in which he dismisses the formal structure of grammar or rules of argumentation as providing power to eloquence: "Our orators have yet to learn that the thing uttered in words is not therefore affirmed. It must affirm itself, or no forms of grammar and no plausibility can give it evidence, and no array of arguments" (*EL* 2: 163). So it was that he would be able to decry "rhetorical rules" that inhibit expression from eloquent language-users (*JMN* 3: 55).

Some of the earliest signs of Emerson's dissatisfaction with the formalism of the belletristic school come in his "On the Best Mode of Inspiring a Correct Taste in English Literature" (1835). While the lecture affirms some of belletrism's basic assumptions about the role of taste in self-culture, it offers an early statement of Emerson's displeasure with some of belletrism's results, a dissatisfaction that surfaces more forcefully only two years later in "The American Scholar." The "taste" of the title explicitly recalls the belletristic keyword that governs interpretation and expression, but Emerson reprimands the young scholars who spend a "barren season of discipline" with writers such as Blair "acquiring the false doctrine that there is something arbitrary or conventional in letters" (*EL* 1: 215). Suspicion over the power of Blair was no doubt on Emerson's mind a year earlier when Thomas Carlyle wrote to him and ruminated on the Scot's work:

> For you are to know, my view is that now at last we have lived to see all manner of Poetics and Rhetorics and Sermonics, and one may say generally all manner of *Pulpits* for addressing mankind from, as good as broken and abolished. . . . [A]nd so one leaves the pasteboard coulisses, and three unities, and Blair's Lectures, quite behind; and feels only that there is *nothing sacred*, then, but the *Speech of Man* to believing Men! (*Correspondence* 104)

Emerson's distaste for Blair might be called a distaste for an educational methodology that stifles the imagination and removes the sacredness from rhetorical acts. Emerson's lecture, embodying a newly rising conception of rhetoric, offers an alternative way of reading in order to ensure creativity and inspiration, not simply mechanical knowledge.

The opening of the lecture is an immediate movement away from the belletristic school: "I confess, Gentlemen, I have not much confidence in the application of any mechanical means to promote a spiritual end. As all the physicians of the world cannot manufacture one drop of blood, neither can all the colleges make one scholar nor the best library a reader" (*EL* 1: 210). The "mechanical means" refer to a way of learning in the colleges that emphasizes rational practicality, and in the following lines, Emerson juxtaposes them with an artificial silence: "If the genius of a country is wholly averse to learning and so warlike, or commercial, or dissolute, that they cannot hear the voice of their wise men I have no hope that any expedients will cure their deafness" (*EL* 1: 210). The deafness to the sounds of genius is a deafness to the "voice of Human Nature" (*EL* 1: 212) that inspires holy scriptures of various cultures. "The genius" and "the scholar," used interchangeably in this lecture (as they are at times in "The American Scholar"), read best when he is not "passive" (*EL* 1: 214) but creates new meaning from old texts. Personal interpretation of literature, then, leaves behind mechanical instruction, a hermeneutical maneuver that implicitly condemns belletristic literary criticism. That condemnation, however, broadens barely two years later in "The American Scholar" to encompass the entirety of the educational system, not just literature.

With the 1837 delivery of "The American Scholar," Emerson breaks definitively with American belletristic rhetoric, marking a significant shift in the rhetorical theory of nineteenth-century America. Indeed, throughout "The American Scholar," Emerson calls on the rhetorical tradition to make his claims for a new American nation, and he attempts to overturn the prevailing American belletristic strain of rhetoric and replace it with a more imaginative one. Emerson's declared separation signifies the creation of a new theory for rhetoric that repudiates American appropriations of belletristic rhetoric and links language with divine ecstasy.

Robert Connors writes that "the romantic movement, important though it is to literary studies and, indeed, to any understanding of the development of European and American culture, has until recently been given little consideration as a force in nineteenth century rhetoric" (302). Indeed, the authors of *Reason to Believe: Romanticism, Pragmatism, and the Teaching of Writing* make this absence the centerpiece of their analysis of American rhetorics. Arguing that American pragmatism as it applies to American educational settings can best be understood as descended of romantic rhetorics, they insist that renewed investigation of the period is needed: "For our purposes, one of the more severe consequences of composition's continuing embrace of the evolutionary metaphor has been the neglect of the connection between North American romanticism, pragmatism, and rhetoric" (105). Among the most central figures of that vein of romanticism is Emerson, who should be considered as foreshadowing "not only the pragmatism of Peirce, James, Dewey, and others, but the studies of cognition and literacy that have influenced composition studies so profoundly in the last thirty years" (56) because, as they argue later, "Emerson's writing . . . becomes his reform action and allows him to work within the tension of word and deed" (62). His work represents "the rhetoric employed by the romantics" that "makes use of self-discovery as a tool for societal recovery and change" (63).

Losing Emerson as a rhetorician has resulted in partial understandings of Emersonian theory as outlined in lectures and essays such as "The American Scholar," which is most often (and reasonably) read as a literary call to arms for a new American state. The audience for this invocation of a new American scholar, however, was grounded in belletristic conceptions of education, so Emerson's lecture tackles not simply the burgeoning literary culture but the burgeoning rhetorical culture as well. Indeed, Emerson likely would not have separated the two, and certainly his audience would not have made the divisions between a new American literary call and a new American rhetorical call that today's audiences might expect: the arts, while distinct, were joined as part of one educational program. So, Emerson's new American scholar is not simply a new literary artist but a new rhetorician. Emerson makes this clear early in the lecture when he invokes concerns typical of belletristic education: "We do not meet for games of strength or skill, for the recitation of histories, tragedies, and odes, like the ancient Greeks; for parliaments of love and poesy, like the Troubadours; nor for the advancement of science, like our contemporaries in the British and European capitals" (*CW* 1: 52). Emerson here confronts modes of learning through historical perspectives, so that the early generations' concerns with declamation are joined with poetry and science in later ones. These broad categories represent different educational strategies—physical, rhetorical, literary, and scientific respectively—and Emerson's point is that the American state has not given proper acknowledgment to training in any of these domains. Instead, the new nation is too concerned with "mechanical skill" (*CW* 1: 52) to the degree that people have been divided up: "The state of society is one in which the members have suffered amputation from the trunk, and strut about so many walking monsters" (*CW* 1: 53).

Combating unnatural division is central to Emerson's project because only by joining different educational concepts can a whole person be realized. In other words, studying rhetoric divorced from other arts leads to monstrous results.

The consequences of severing educational programs from each other are made clear in Emerson's discussion of the scholar's use of books. After establishing the importance of nature to the scholar and describing the scholar's work as unifying nature through classifying the world (Emerson defines classification as "perceiving that these objects are not chaotic, and are not foreign" [*CW* 1: 54]), he argues that books should be used for the creation of new ideas. Without new creation, the scholar is simply a bookworm divorced from the divine: "Whatever talents may be, if the man create not, the pure efflux of the Deity is not his;—cinders and smoke there may be, but not yet flame" (*CW* 1: 57). The flame imagery here is significant because Emerson returns to it time and again throughout his career in describing the power of the imagination and creative expression to transcend the material world to the divine. That material world is represented by the belletristic demand for imitation that was required of young scholars in Emerson's time; so Emerson's repudiation of imitation here overturns American appropriations of Blair's *imitatio.*

Throughout the section on "books," rhetoric or eloquence is only referred to obliquely, but in the section on "action," eloquence is invoked to illustrate the point that overcoming the material world results in profound divine activity. Action is the fuel for eloquence: "It is pearls and rubies to his discourse. Drudgery, calamity, exasperation, want, are instructors in eloquence and wisdom. The true scholar grudges every opportunity of action past [*sic*] by, as a loss of power" (*CW* 1: 59). The material obstacles to discourse are transformed into pearls and rubies, so that even the most dull or painful become movement to power. The joining of action, eloquence, and wisdom signifies a deliberate reconfiguration of American belletristic rhetoric that becomes most apparent as he defines how the scholar is supposed to act in the world.

Emerson outlines the duties of the American scholar in rhetorical terms that his audience would have quickly recognized: "The office of the scholar is to cheer, to raise, and to guide men by showing them facts amid appearances" (*CW* 1: 62).[5] Emerson, here, recapitulates Cicero's classical purposes of the rhetoric, which are to delight, to teach, and to move. They are presumed in Blair's work and most American rhetorical handbooks, but they are rarely yoked to Emerson's final phrase "by showing them facts amid appearances." Such a phrase places Emerson squarely in a long tradition of Platonic rhetoric, which requires that the rhetor move the audience beyond appearances and to transcendental truth. By relying on the universality of creative expression, Emerson is able to join all the belletristic arts together, so that the poet's words are most universal when he is alone and records his most private thoughts, and the orator can best move his audience by relying on the deeply personal: "The deeper he dives into his privatest, secretest presentiment, to his wonder he finds this is the most acceptable, most public, and universally true" (*CW* 1: 63). The personal here, as in most of Emerson's work, becomes the most universal.

Frederick Antczak, borrowing from Kenneth Burke, has called this a "rhetoric of identification" (126) in that the individual's goal in communication is identification between self and audience. Antczak, however, prioritizes the role of the individual to a degree that it disregards the civic life, a proposition contrary to Emerson's argument. The point of Emerson's discussion of the individual is to move from the deeply personal to the universal, a maneuver that is contrary to American belletristic rhetoric, which requires both imitation of models and a highly formalized and structured sense of audience.

In fact, most rhetoric handbooks of the time recommend repeated lessons in imitation of great orations and recurring drilling in audience considerations. Emerson rejects these exercises; indeed, he suggests that a focus on imitation and audience leads to a misunderstanding of issues at hand. Instead, speakers should break open the shallow sense of audience with a view toward deeper, more powerful forces at work:

> The human mind cannot be enshrined in a person who shall set a barrier on any one side to this unbounded, unboundable empire. It is one central fire, which, flaming now out of the lips of Etna, lightens the capes of Sicily, and now out of the throat of Vesuvius, illuminates the towers and vineyards of Naples. It is one light which beams out of a thousand stars. It is one soul which animates all men. (*CW* 1: 66)

The personification of volcanoes with images of the mouth here illustrates the way in which the scholar/poet/orator quite literally speaks by a universal fire running beneath the surfaces of things. Its power is unceasing and boundless.

"Eloquence" and the Flames of the Imagination

Emerson's later lecture on "Eloquence" (1867) stands as one of his lengthiest ruminations on the power of rhetoric, and in it, he explicitly links this flaming undercurrent of power with the imagination and, in turn, with social action. In discussing the eloquent power of the commoner living in "some lowly Bethel," he argues that contact with Nature allows the lowly man to "[pour] out the abundant streams of his thought through a language all glittering and fiery with imagination." This is a man "whom college drill or patronage never made" and whose only lessons are from "the torrent in the gloom of the pinewoods, when he was the companion of the mountain cattle, of jays and foxes" (*CW* 8: 60). Imaginative expression emerges from a connection with nature that leads to fiery imaginative expression, not unlike that expected of the American scholar.

To a far greater degree than in "The American Scholar," however, flame and fire images dominate "Eloquence"; the increasing use of such graphic imagery in the later work testifies to Emerson's rising despair over the materialism and mechanistic quality of American educational and vocational culture. Emerson's changing attitudes about the public sphere for rhetoric and indeed about his own vocation as a public speaker have been widely discussed, most lucidly by Mary Kupiec Cayton in recent years, but starting in some notable ways with Stephen Whicher's classic, if now less widely consulted, analysis of Emerson in *Freedom and Fate*. Both demonstrate Emerson's frustration with an America that had turned toward a noxious materialism. The images of the later "Eloquence" lecture, then, are linked directly to a new type of imaginative expression that transcends the false and mechanical oratory that Emerson implicitly condemns and personally loathed.

In an opening discussion of forensic and legislative rhetoric, Emerson argues that eloquence has impact beyond mere rules of expression: "The facts, the reasons, the logic,—above all, the flame of passion and the continuous energy of will which is presently to be let loose on this bench of judges, or on this miscellaneous assembly gathered from the streets,—all are invisible and unknown" (*CW* 8: 59). While Emerson here invokes the typical standards of belletristic instruction, "the facts, the reasons, the logic," he asserts the superiority of an unquantifiable and virtually ineffable force that makes rhetoric powerful. This force is not reason but something deeper.

For Emerson, this deep power is the equivalent of action. Recalling again the formulation he first proposes in "The American Scholar," Emerson argues that "his [the 'true orator's'] speech is not to be distinguished from action. It is the electricity of action. It is action, as the general's word of command, or chart of battle, is action" (*CW* 8: 61). This electric action is powerful because it lights up and heats "the cold and malicious assembly" through an act of "prophecy" that wins an audience that "expected repetition" (*CW* 8: 62). The contrast of electric power and cold assembly hall parallels the contrast between prophecy and repetition and illustrates the way in which the true orator's divine power overwhelms an audience taught to expect a specific sort of rehearsed oratory. While Emerson appreciates the skills necessary to hone belletristic oratory, he minimizes those skills in the face of natural expression. For example, immediately after describing the power of the true orator to quite literally light up the room with electric heat, he describes the "ingredients" of eloquence: "clear perceptions; memory; power of statement; logic; imagination, or the skill to clothe your thought in natural images; passion, which is the *heat*; and then a grand will, which, when legitimate and abiding, we call *character*, the height of manhood" (*CW* 8: 62). The earliest ingredients are well-known and expected qualities of oratory that are espoused throughout American belletristic rhetoric; Newman, as the central example of antebellum American belletristic rhetoric, addresses most of them in his work, often under considerations of style and arrangement. The last three, however, are contested terms: some, like passion, are shackled by belletristic theories. Indeed, imagination, passion, and will are linked in the list by Emerson's attempts to define the terms and raise them to divine expression. Nature, the central feature of the imagination in this list, is the metaphor for divinity that animates the fiery undercurrent of passion and will.

Emerson's inversion of the list of eloquence's ingredients continues throughout the essay. Emerson argues that "the language of the street" is superior "to that of the academy," chastising Lord Chesterfield, the ultimate example of tasteful expression endorsed by the belletrists, for believing that only the "*Halles*" can provide rich and powerful expression (*CW* 8: 66). Indeed, the lessons learned in unnatural places such as the academy are "the gymnastics, the education of eloquence, and not itself." They provide certain skills (which may be necessary) but cannot substitute for the imagination, the passions, and the will. Instead, all men, regardless of education, when moved to "a great heat" can "express themselves with an almost equal force" (*CW* 8: 67). In an earlier published version of the essay, Emerson goes even further, enumerating key traits only to dismiss them in favor of a core principle: "a good voice, winning manners, plain speech, chastened, however, by the schools into correctness." But these "ascending stairs" remain subordinate to knowledge of the deep laws and facts of the universe: "Know your fact; hug your fact. For the essential thing is heat, and heat comes of sincerity" (*W* 8: 129–30). The "fact" Emerson invokes here is truth, however personal, and it generates a heat that is the essential element of rhetoric. The other qualities—voice and plain speech from the second list and logic and reasons from the first—are the mechanical tools that aid in the ascension, but they are not the essential element. Heat from the passions expressed with the imagination is. Emerson describes the imaginative heat earlier in the essay when discussing a speaker who seems incompetent in personal dialogue but rises to greatness in oratory:

> What is peculiar in it is a certain creative heat, which a man attains to perhaps only once in his life. Those whom we admire—the great orators—have some *habit* of heat, and moreover, a certain control of it, an art of husbanding it,—as if their hand was on the organ-stop, and could now use it temperately, and now let out all the length and breadth of the power. (*CW* 8: 63)

This creative force, which raises the divine through the use of imagination, comes only through a "deep interest or sympathy" that "thaws the ice, loosens the tongue, and will carry the cold and fearful presently into self-possession and possession of the audience" (*CW* 8: 63). Self-possession, knowing one's fact, and assertion of the will are interdependent, and each leads to an overwhelming imaginative and persuasive heat in eloquence. Great orators make a habit of marshaling this heat.

Deliberately firing the imagination directly confronts American belletristic rhetoric because the imagination need not abide by reason-centered invention and expression of formal expression. In his earlier lecture on "Eloquence" (1847), Emerson begins his discussion of rhetoric by appealing to individual temperaments, whether highly rational or highly emotional, to demonstrate that each person differs "in capacity of heat, or, we boil at different degrees" (*W* 7: 61), and are thus inclined to different kinds of eloquence. Emerson argues that regardless of an individual's capacity for rational argumentation, the finest rhetoric is sometimes entirely disconnected from reason: "That which he wishes, that which eloquence ought to reach, is not a particular skill in telling a story, or neatly summing up evidence, or arguing logically . . . no, but a taking sovereign possession of the audience" (*W* 7: 65). Assuming complete control of the audience entails an understanding of the divine that transcends rhetorical rules and systems. This transcendence he calls "personal ascendancy," and he declares that it is a key feature of rhetoric:

> Eloquence is the appropriate organ of the highest personal energy. Personal ascendency may exist with or without adequate talent for its expression. It is as surely felt as a mountain or a planet; but when it is weaponed with a power of speech, it seems first to become truly human, works actively in all directions, and supplies the imagination with fine materials. (*W* 7: 81)

"Personal ascendency," here, is an Emersonian expression for individual connection to divinity, and that connection ensures the infusion of imaginative rhetoric with "fine materials." Emerson insists that such power emerges not just in speech but in written eloquence as well. In his manuscript notes for the lecture, he writes, "The word Eloquence strictly means *outspeaking*, *outcry*, and yet we often speak of eloquent writing: and we always use the word to express a certain heat or spasm of feeling, which surprises us in the usual level tone of solitary writing" (bMs Am 1280.199, folder 2, p. 26). Elsewhere he invokes George Herbert to make the point that this heat is not generated from method but elevation of the soul:

> I often make the criticism on my friend Herbert's diction that his thought has that heat as actually to fuse the words so that language is wholly flexible in his hands & his rhyme never stops the progress of sense. And, in general, according to the elevation of the soul will the power over language always be, & lively thoughts will break out into spritely verse. No measure so difficult but will be tractable so that you only get up the temperature of the thought[.] To this point I quote gladly my old gossip Montaigne "For my part I hold, & Socrates is positive in it, That whoever has in his mind a spritely & clear imagination, he will express it well enough in one kind or another, & tho' he were dumb[,] by signs." (*JMN* 3: 284)

Divine inspiration supplies an imaginative rhetoric with the necessary tools for expression so that rhetorical education can, at least in part, be left behind.

Historicizing Emerson's Resistance to Belletristic Rhetorics

Emerson's resistance to the dominant trends in nineteenth-century rhetorical education should not be read as a simplistic and sustained attack on Blair and the Scottish New Rhetorics. Indeed, while he attacked Blair early in his career, in his later "Eloquence" lecture he cites Blair as a model for instruction in propriety of speech (*W* 8: 117). Similarly, Dugald Stewart offered Emerson a vocabulary for articulating an innate moral sense that is central to his invocation of a deep and abiding heat necessary for true eloquence. Blair, of course, shares this with Stewart, but Stewart's *Elements of the Philosophy of the Human Mind* provided a philosophical language for an interior moral compass that would draw together internal reflection and civic action. For Stewart, Lockean sensationalism had concrete limitations including, among other things, the role of the imagination in shaping human character. The imagination increases sensibility to human suffering, so that a lack of sympathy with fellow humans indicates a fundamental lack of imagination: "I have often been inclined to think, that the apparent coldness and selfishness of mankind may be traced, in a great measure, to a want of attention and a want of imagination" (*Elements* 433). Even so, Stewart is careful to warn that the imagination be reined in by reason, or else every sort of moral turpitude, such as sexual promiscuity or alcoholism, might ensue (443). For Stewart, there must be a systematic educational program in place so that reason is taught as central to the exercise of the imagination (31–35). This systematic education, as Stewart would outline in other works, would teach taste and would be governed by a "power of analytic discrimination or discernment in the examination of its appropriate objects" (*Works* 334).

Emerson draws from Stewart the elevation of civic duty and the power of the imagination, which Stewart says is best exercised in the fine arts, especially literature and painting. Indeed, both Emerson and the belletrists link the fine arts to action so that Emerson shares with Blair and Stewart an idealism grounded in civic responsibility. What Emerson sought to transcend was the limitations of rhetorical action by a reason-obsessed rhetoric.

This transcendence can best be understood, then, not as a repudiation of Blair or other belletrists, explicitly, but as a challenge to New England educational appropriations of them. While Scottish belletristic rhetoric maintains a concern with moral action, New England theorists translated the New Rhetorics into a set of rules for propriety, a series of exercises emphasizing the imitation of models, and a system of proper speaking and writing that evolved into standardizations governing the lecture circuit. The modeling behavior, of course, would not sit particularly well with the Emerson of "The American Scholar," and he would ultimately reshape it in the same way that he would reconceive of poetry: engage the imagination and experience the ecstasy of the divine.

Emerson's concern with building an imaginative and revelatory rhetoric, then, is as much a concern with discarding authoritative, rationalistic, and empiricist dictums for action and the ways of knowing that they communicated to their audience as it is a formulation of a new rhetoric. He was aiming for revolution, and he found it in the power of the imagination to move people to act in the world. A comparison he makes early in his life when, in a discussion about eloquence, he compares himself to the mysterious and mythical leader of Britain's Cade rebellion, is instructive: "Jack Cade was not more inclined to proscribe grammar from his domains than I method from mine. . . . Eloquence is best inspired by an Infinite Cause. It is always an agreeable picture to the human imagination, to the allusions to the strength of seeming weakness" (*JMN* 2: 318–19). He develops this line of thinking in more detail throughout his life: "The blundering rhetorician seeks in the tones rising & falling inflexions, or in the gestures of Chatham or Adams, or in the circumstances of the parties present or concerned, the electricity that lay only in the breast of Chatham & Adams, *Pectus est disertum et vis mentis*" (*JMN* 4: 429).[6] The final phrase is from Quintilian's *Institutes of Oratory* and translates to "For it is feeling and force of imagination that makes us eloquent." The point, here, is that copying the external signs of eloquence or trying to form a model or method by which eloquence can be gained is impossible because that power comes only from the internal heat of an individual's imagination. That he invokes William Chatham and John Adams should be no surprise, as their oratory was revered because it roused the masses to act. It fostered civic action.

Equally important, as early as 1836, the year he would publish his first major work, *Nature*, Emerson recognizes one of the root causes of the quiet, insidious forces of the status quo: the Common Sense school of rhetoric. He notes that cultural obligation to that school of thought is driven by all manner of worldly evils, and he calls for a rebellion:

> Observe how strongly guarded is the Common Sense. If men were left to Contemplation, if the contemplative life were practicable[,] to what subtilties [*sic*] to what dreams & extravagancies would not all run! Laputa, a court of love, a college of Schoolmen, would be the result. How is this hindered? Poverty, Frost, Famine, Rain, Disease are the beadles & guardsmen that hold us to Common Sense. (*JMN* 5: 217)

Because rhetoric is so intimately related to action, as it is in these journal entries and works like "The American Scholar," and because rhetoric is so closely connected to spirituality, as the fire imagery illustrates in the later "Eloquence" lecture, Emerson's rhetoric should be read as enacting a new paradigm for rhetorical power: rhetoric brings reform through the individual soul. Our fear of things like poverty and famine keep us wedded to our old ways of acting and speaking, and yet they offer no viable course to create change. A new rhetoric would foster new ways of being in the world, and to do so, it must undermine the systematic and formal rhetorics of belletristic America. American belletrism, hobbled by rules of expression, is impotent, and only an intuitive rhetoric birthed from the imagination provides the energy necessary for revolution in culture.

Emerson returns to this notion even late in life, and when he does, he goes so far as to link it to the rhetoric of the person who first defined rhetoric for him, Plato:

> I think the Platonists may be read for sentences,—though the reader fail to grasp the argument of the paragraph or chapter. He may yet obtain gleams and glimpses of a more excellent illumination from their genius, outvaluing the most distinct information he owes to other books. For I hold that the grandeur of the impression the stars and heavenly bodies make on us, is surely more valuable than our exact perception of a tub or a table on the ground. (*LL* 2: 234)

Emerson here finds in Platonism the same traits that he valorizes in "Eloquence." Systems of understanding, logical arrangement, coherence of argument—none provide the impact of the gleams from the sentences. Indeed, they seem virtually irrelevant in comparison to the power of the epiphanic sentence, as Emerson links them to "a tub or a table on the ground" whose significance clearly pales in comparison to the stars in the heavens.

Emerson ultimately replaces rules with the imagination, arguing for the imaginative faculty's centrality in transforming an entire society. With the imagination at the center of the rhetorical act, rhetoric is conflated with other forms of imaginative discourse, and even philosophical dialogue. Though recalling the belletristic impulse to link literary and rhetorical expression, Emerson nonetheless breaks from belletrist formalism to suggest a divine power working in the literary artist and the rhetor. Language, then, becomes a vehicle for divine will, and both poetics and rhetoric become vehicles of social change.

5. EMERSON'S PANHARMONICON AND THE SOUNDS OF A NEW LECTURE

Ronald Bosco and Joel Myerson's *Later Lectures of Ralph Waldo Emerson* opens with an invitation to begin a new path for Emerson scholarship. The editors contend that a full study of Emerson as a lecturer has yet to be written and that our scholarship on Emerson as orator has not yet matched Emerson's reputation as a speaker during his lifetime. Four years later, Bosco and Myerson echo the same call for more work in this area in the introduction to their *Selected Lectures of Ralph Waldo Emerson*, even as they develop a clearer picture of Emerson's vocation in the pages that follow. They identify four primary reasons (up from three in the introduction of *The Later Lectures*) that Emerson's lecture career has received less attention than other aspects of his career, and they note provocatively (usefully so) that "lecturing styles in the mid-nineteenth century were classical in origin, formal in practice, Latinate rather than Saxon in word choice, and long in delivery. Elocution, not ideas, was the standard of the day, and Emerson was always dubious of its value" (xvi). The observation is useful in that it summarizes precisely some of the key issues Emerson was up against when he began his work as a lecturer. It is provocative because it points researchers to the roots of that lecture career even though it does not explicitly name them. These roots can be found in the rhetorical tradition.

While the purpose of this monograph has not been to trace Emerson's career as a lecturer, it has nonetheless identified aspects of rhetorical theory that are fundamental to understanding Emerson's fascination with and career in oratory. I have argued that Emerson's thinking about rhetoric was deeply informed by central texts in the history of rhetoric and that he considered rhetoric on its own terms, calling on a lineage of orators and rhetorical theorists. Those theorists shaped, for Emerson, a view of rhetoric as a type of action, one with special possibilities in the New Republic because it provided a means to respect and encourage diverse expression while simultaneously dwelling in a divine unity that might otherwise be inaccessible. Only by acting in the world and coming into contact with that variety could a person hope to experience transcendence. To no small degree, Emerson saw his lecturing as a way to act in the world.

Understanding his vision of rhetoric, therefore, would be incomplete without some consideration of Emerson's life as a lecturer and his theorizing of the role of the podium in public life. Lecturing was action in the public sphere, and Emerson not only embraced it but also found in it the possibility of something greater than other modes of expression. Emerson's wide-ranging engagement with rhetorical history and theory led him to conceive of rhetoric as both linked to transcendental principles and highly resistant to simplistic systemization. Indeed, the former requires the latter, as Emerson insists throughout his career that truth and the unification of ideals can only be enacted through free and open expression of diverse voices. Variety is, in this formulation, necessary for unity, and in nineteenth-century America, the extensive varieties of experiences within the rapidly changing demography needed, for Emerson, some principle to bring them together.

Emerson understands the podium as a place to explore the diverse epistemologies that, taken together, paint a fuller picture of transcendence and its capacity to drive change in a society. Instead of imposing a necessary structure or system that would try to encapsulate each possible idea, Emerson formulates a worldview that requires diversity in order to gain a clearer vision of an impossibly expansive core. To embrace diverse voices and visions of that core was to embrace the immensity of it. While Emerson's feeling about the podium changed as he became increasingly frustrated with its strictures and audience expectations, his frustration should be read as an endorsement of the possibility, albeit in his mind a failed one, of the podium to launch a revolution and drive American exceptionalism. The podium's failure, as I will argue, was its increasing drift toward a formalism that limited free expression of ideas. This would not be a new concern of Emerson's.

Emerson's idealizing of the podium can, in part, be read within the framework of specific contingencies that drove Emerson to it. His departure from the church and his need for an ongoing source of income pointed him to the podium as a vocation. His detailed records of lecture fees, including those that were delinquent, illustrate that Emerson's fantasies of a revolution were tempered by the demands of his day. The public intellectual still needed to get paid, even if he was hoping to kindle fervor for new ideas in his audience.

Nonetheless, Emerson dreamed of making a difference through public speaking, and his ascendance in the lecture circuit provided him with the perfect vehicle for the dissemination of his ideas. The history of Emerson scholarship demonstrates an awareness of the large role the podium played in his life, and while the purpose of this chapter is not to finally fill the gap Bosco and Myerson identify in relation to the textual and reception history of his lectures, it nevertheless aims to fill a different gap, one created by disciplinary fractures that have yet to be bridged. This chapter delineates some reasons why Emerson's role as an orator has been relegated to the margins of academic inquiry and offers theoretical grounding from which future scholarship might proceed. It attempts to demonstrate precisely why understanding Emerson as a rhetor, as opposed to an essayist-in-the-making or a philosophical sage, is important. Put more precisely, it argues that understanding rhetorical history is necessary to plumb the depths of Emerson's impact on oratorical culture.

Emersonian Scholarship, Rhetoric, and Disciplinary Identities

The question in front of us, ultimately, is not whether Emerson should be considered an orator and lecturer but how we map him as one. Excluding studies of Emerson in the pulpit, some attempts have already been made. Early on, Herbert Wilchens and, of course, Kenneth Cameron provided useful assessments of Emerson as a speaker, and even F. O. Matthiessen insisted that Emerson's lecturing was central to his vision of himself. In recent decades, Mary Kupiec Cayton, Sallee Engstrom, and Nancy Craig Simmons have provided the much-needed archival legwork to ground theoretical postulations, and scholars like David Robinson and R. Jackson Wilson have offered studies of Emerson's lecturing through the lens of both literary and communication studies. Yet these have been largely starting grounds, if for no other reason than that a book-length treatment has yet to be written on Emerson's oratory and lecturing within the field from which those arts emerge: rhetoric.

Scholars in rhetoric have not, however, been altogether silent. Broad agreement exists that Emerson is central to the American rhetorical scene, and since James Berlin's treatment of him, he has enjoyed more recognition. John Sloan and Roberta Ray each investigate specific elements of Emerson's rhetorical theory within the lectures, such as his view of the audience or the orator, and Ralph LaRosa argues that Lord Bacon was "a source of quotations and rhetorical theory" who "first taught Emerson 'how to shape journal notes into a rounded form'" (108). Nonetheless, rhetoricians have been loath to characterize him as a theorist, or even consider him as part of the rhetorical tradition. When one considers remarks like Bronson Alcott's that "'there was no public lecture till Emerson made it,'" and that "'the lyceums are properly called *Emersonia*, and we must substitute the founder's name for the thing he has invented'" (qtd. in Field 471), the general absence seems especially glaring. Rhetorical studies have yet to fully account for Emerson's—and, more broadly, romanticism's—deep and lasting impact on American conceptions of language in the public sphere.

While I have attended in various places throughout this book to literary scholarship's silence about the distinct intellectual tradition of rhetoric and rhetorical studies, rhetorical scholarship has similarly failed to engage with Emerson as one of its own, creating significant gaps in our understanding of American rhetorical theory. Certainly any understanding of Emerson as a public speaker requires exploration of the rhetorical tradition in order to offer the richest and fullest accounting of Emerson's view of the podium—to do otherwise would be to leave out the millennia-old theorizing that essentially paved the way for the American lecture circuit—but so too does our understanding of antebellum rhetoric require fuller engagement with romantic rhetorics like Emerson's. One would not, by analogy, expect a full examination of Emerson's poetry without some grounding in a history and culture of poetics. Similarly, Emerson's view of the natural world is best informed when it takes into account the rise of the natural sciences during the eighteenth and nineteenth centuries. And so it is with Emerson's lecturing: understanding Emerson as lecturer necessitates fuller engagement with the rhetorical tradition, and rhetorical history is more accurately reported when it includes theories that do not align with rhetorical "systems."[1]

This is not to say previous scholarship misrepresents Emerson's project. Emerson's message to make meaningful changes to cultural institutions is remarkably consistent across his career, and both literary and rhetorical scholars have recognized that. Instead, it suggests only that our understanding of nineteenth-century American public culture is incomplete because one of the most important influences on it has been lost.

Rhetorical history shaped Emersonian expression just as Emerson in turn shaped rhetorical theory, and while other influences are surely essential and enriching in making sense of both, the absence of rhetoric—as a field of study, a set of theories and epistemologies, and a system of delivery—in Emerson studies, especially, has made understanding Emerson as a lecturer virtually impossible. While scholars have connected Emerson to obscure linguists, marginal philosophers, and surprisingly distant poets—all in fascinating and helpful ways—the most obvious tradition to mine for understanding lecturing has been largely ignored. We have, in other words, sequestered Emerson so firmly within the literary canon that some of the more obvious relationships have been effectively erased.

The reasons for this, of course, are complex. Individual interests and disciplinary identities shape scholarship, as do disciplinary disputes and scholarly squabbles.[2] Nonetheless, the interest of recent scholars in expanding our understanding of Emerson's impact provides an opportunity to reconsider his legacy in both literary and rhetorical studies. The increased scholarship on Emerson in political science is an example of this, as is the way in which Emerson's writings have been examined in light of the sciences more and more. Similarly, the Emerson Society has actively sponsored novel research agendas that reach across the proverbial aisle, and it maintains a tradition of expansive thinking, befitting its namesake. Given the reemergence of rhetoric as a field within the academy, rhetorical readings of Emerson are possible in ways now that were unthinkable even twenty years ago.

Emerson as Lecturer

The editors of Emerson's *Early Lectures* provide a particularly useful framework for Emerson's early reckoning with the lecture circuit. Juxtaposing Emerson's move to Concord in 1835 with Emerson's journal entries leading up to his first lecture series, Stephen Whicher, Robert Spiller, and Wallace Williams draw attention to Emerson's preoccupation with what it meant to be a podium speaker:

> "I design not to utter any speech, poem or book that is not entirely and peculiarly my work. I will say at public lectures, and the like, those things which I have meditated for their own sake, and not for the first time with a view to that occasion." "'Remember,' he cautions himself as he sets out to prepare the new series in

> December [1834], 'you are not to say, What must be said in a Lyceum? but, What discoveries or stimulating thoughts have I to impart to a thousand persons? not what they will expect to hear, but what is fit for me to say.'" (*EL* 1: 93)

Even this early in Emerson's career (and, for that matter, in the life of the American Lyceum), however, Emerson was "becoming dissatisfied both with the restraints imposed by the lyceum system and with the subject of science as there presented" (*EL* 1: 93). This displeasure only grew over time. In 1840, he wrote that

> these lectures give me little pleasure. I have not done what I hoped when I said, I will try it once more. I have not once transcended the coldest selfpossession. I said I will agitate others, being agitated myself. . . . Alas! alas! I have not the recollection of one strong moment. (*JMN* 8: 338–39)

Similarly, as he was near the end of his career, he lamented in a somewhat infamous passage in his journals, "Why has never the poorest country college offered me a professorship of rhetoric? I think I could have taught an orator, though I am none" (*JMN* 15: 246).

Emerson's sense of self-doubt has been widely discussed, from Stephen Whicher to Randall Fuller, and more extensively by Kay Jamison, who argues that Emerson struggled with depression and that his creative output should be read in light of that struggle.[3] Nonetheless, Emerson held special hope for the lyceum, one based on the profound democratic possibilities it afforded in advancing a culture's embrace of higher laws:

> But a field for eloquence higher and deeper seems to me already opened in the Lyceum, an institution now in its infancy, yet growing every year into use and favor in the Atlantic cities. . . . It answers the purpose of a social meeting for both sexes in a very convenient manner, involving no expense, and no dissipation . . . and so supplants the theatre and the ballroom. . . . But these are the beginnings of its use. I set a higher value on it than amusement or the statement of valuable facts. I look upon it as a vent for new and higher communications than any to which we have been wont to listen. . . .
>
> For this is precisely the most elastic and capacious theatre of eloquence,—absolutely unrestricted. (*LL* 1: 47–48)

The transformation of the lecture hall from simply amusement or practical instruction in "facts" into a place for "unrestricted" expression and thought is its greatest possibility. Emerson saw in the lyceum a place where an entire culture could be awakened to greater truths because it had "less strict conventions than other assemblies or pulpits,—and [could] invite, perhaps a bolder exercise of thought" (*LL* 1: 49). Indeed, Emerson reveled in the possibility not only of the lyceum itself but also the lyceum lecture as a form of expression: "With all deference to the lovers of precision and method, I think that the best method will always be a new one, new with each speaker, and proper to that which he has to say" (*LL* 1: 49). Emerson here explicitly jettisons method, arguing that lecture propriety inhibits true expression, one that will "excite the slumbering intellect, make it a party to the speaker's thought, and by hints and whispers even, if no more can be . . . leave it with a renewed assurance that that world exists—and for him" (*LL* 1: 49). This ecstatic vision, one that might come even simply through "hints and whispers," requires a place that allows for unrestricted access and expression. Further, it is place that must embrace new method, one unique to each speaker. With each new expression, Emerson hoped for "enchantment" (*LL* 1: 48).

Emerson explicitly wedded that hope to American identity. In journal entries from which he drew to compose some of the earlier passages, Emerson links it to national identity and to the metaphor he would repeatedly use to represent the new lecture "method":

> Why should we write dramas, & epics, & sonnets, & novels in two volumes? Why not write as variously as we dress & think? A lecture is a new literature, which leaves aside all tradition, time, place, circumstance, & addresses an assembly as mere human beings,—no more—It has never yet been done well. It is an organ of sublime power[,] a panharmonicon for variety of note. But only then is the orator successful when he is himself agitated & is as much a hearer as any of the assembly. In that office you may & shall (please God!) yet see the electricity part from the cloud & shine from one part of heaven to the other. (*JMN* 7: 224–25)

Emerson's invocation of electricity as the power of the lecture connects it to a special form of imaginative expression that, for Emerson, trumps well-worn models of literature.[4] The new literature, reflecting the diversity of sounds from a panharmonicon, better represents the core of American identity. Discard the old forms, Emerson exhorts some of his peers; the lecture is all our own.

The image of the panharmonicon, invoked in Emerson's journal entry and then transplanted into his lecture "Genius, Manners, and Customs" (*LL* 1: 48), is central to Emerson's view of the lecture, and I discuss it in more detail later in this chapter, but here, Emerson emphasizes the capacity of the lecture to be something entirely new, something extraordinary. It "leaves aside all tradition, time, place, circumstance," and offers speakers the opportunity to not only change the assembly but themselves as well.

Sallee Engstrom astutely situates Emerson's hope for this new literature within a culture that was seeking new modes of expression, and she points out that Emerson was not the only one to argue that the lecture was an American literature. She cites E. P. Whipple, who argues in the *Christian Review* that

> "in the present age the popular lecture occupies a very important sphere and cannot properly be overlooked in estimating the influences at work in society. It clearly comes within the range of periodical literature[;] . . . [lectures] present in a sprightly and attractive style such view of literature and life as are of common or universal interest." (qtd. in Engstrom 62)

The "universal interest" of the lecture would surely have appealed to Emerson, and his career in the podium suggests, despite his moments of doubt, that he believed that something revolutionary could emerge in that space.

Emerson's lecturing should be read as a rejection of both the literary and the oratorical conventions of his day. Indeed his peripatetic style is perhaps best understood as an attempt to circumvent the strictures of the lyceum as much as, if not more than, the constraints on literary modes of expression. He argues against standard homiletics in a similar way that he would with lecturing:

> I cannot hear a sermon without being struck by the fact that amid drowsy series of sentences what a sensation a historical fact, a biographical name, a sharply objective illustration makes! Why will not the preacher heed the admonition of the silence momentary of his congregation & (often what is shown him) that this particular sentence is all they carry away? (*JMN* 5: 197)

Here, Emerson posits the centrality of the sentence in stunning an audience to silence, and he would develop this idea as a centerpiece to his rhetoric. Reflecting on the courage it takes to confront an idea directly and "march up to it & sit down before it" he suggests that lecturing can help an audience to face hard truths head on:

> A lecture may be given upon insects or plants, that, when it is closed, irresistibly suggests the question, "Well, what of that?" An enumeration of facts without method. A true method has no more need of firstly, secondly, &c. than a perfect sentence has of punctuation. It tells its own story, makes its own feet, creates its own form. It is its own apology. The best argument of the lawyer is a skillful telling of the story. (*JMN* 4: 290)

Here, Emerson connects the precision of the natural sciences with the precision of a new form of lecture. No list is needed, and neither is a system of classification or order of delivery to reach the truth of the matter. Instead, it "creates its own form," and even the smallest unit of expression, the sentence, needs no rules to contain it.

Emerson's mode of expression, which moves from aphorism to aphorism and eschews traditional rhetorical arrangement, embraces this vision of meaning and purpose for language. The sentence, the small gem of expression, that animates his lectures derives from a belief that formal systems failed to capture the essence of a thing. This belief undoubtedly owes something to a wide range of forces on Emerson's craft—from biblical sententiae, to poetics, to the essay genre, to Eastern notions of revelatory expression—but it was the podium that provided Emerson with the contingency to test his new ways of knowing and expressing his ideas. As Sandra Gustafson points out, Emerson's writing served the creation of his lectures and fostered his growth as an orator, not the other way around (276). He wrote lectures. He compiled essays.

When Emerson's style is considered to be a result of his attempts to revolutionize the podium, we are confronted with the fact that it responded to a very specific historical occasion—rhetorical culture and the rise of the lyceum in antebellum America. To divorce Emerson's trademark style from that moment is to fundamentally miss how revolutionary it is. Indeed, it misses how Emerson consciously tried to form a mode of delivery that would, on the one hand, escape the formalism of the lyceum while, on the other hand, inspire audiences to embrace and even create new ideas.

David Robinson provides a useful exploration of Emerson as a lecturer and focuses, at times, on his trademark style. Robinson situates Emerson's lecture career as a kind of pivot point between his life as a preacher and his life as a writer, positing that the lecture helped Emerson rethink his vocation. As Emerson moved from the pulpit toward a career as essayist, Robinson notes that Emerson "benefited enormously from one sociological phenomenon in his lifetime—the rising popularity of the public lecture." And while Robinson is careful to acknowledge the impact the public podium had on Emerson by giving him an audience to hear his ideas, Robinson suggests that the lecture circuit provided him, nearly above all other things, "a rare opportunity for Emerson to embrace the more literary side of the ministerial vocation, leaving aside its pastoral aspects" (71). "For Emerson," Robinson writes, "the lectures form an invaluable bridge from the pursuit of preacher to that of essayist," acknowledging that "it was largely through his repeated use of the series of interconnected lectures that he molded something like a philosophical system. It was also a version of this form which gave shape to his major literary accomplishment, the collected series of essays of the 1840s and 1850s" (72). Robinson argues that Emerson's increasing dissatisfaction with the podium parallels his dissatisfaction with the pulpit and drives him to essay writing: "Out of the growing disillusionment with the spoken word, Emerson turned with increasing expectation toward the written word." His written words, however, "were formed largely from the legacy of his ambition for the lecture," and the essays accordingly contain "a blend of oratorical flair, confession, conversational chattiness, and aphorism" (160–61). Robinson's assessment, which becomes clearest in the final pages of his book, is that Emerson's writing is essentially grounded on homiletic forms, and he implies that Emerson's lecturing and his ideas about oratory are effectively momentary departures from a continuity of thinking from his early career to his late. Lecturing, in this assessment, is secondary to Emerson's initial ideas about self-culture and the individual, and indeed is a kind of weigh station on his path toward literary genius.

The problem, of course, is that Emerson lectured throughout his lifetime, and his thinking about oratory, eloquence, and rhetoric is a significant part of his broader philosophical thoughts on American culture. The lecture as a form—no matter how frustrated Emerson became with it—remained a primary method of communication for him, and he was self-consciously concerned with understanding and describing how it worked, making explicit comments on rhetoric even late in his career. Robinson's formulation, even with its insightful discussions of the relationship between Emerson's sense of vocation and his philosophical and literary yearnings, treats this aspect of Emerson's work as secondary to his literary development as an essayist. This is not to say Emerson was not concerned with developing a literary style, as Robinson carefully traces, but to find in Emerson's lectures only signs of literary genius or cultural savvy around print culture is to miss entirely Emerson's deliberate attempt to rethink the power of the podium and the way that power could best be enacted. Robinson points out that to understand Emerson's "very real innovations" in "thought and expression" we need "fuller recourse to those foundations" against which he was rebelling (184), and yet the most significant of those foundations in terms of lecturing—rhetorical history—is entirely absent from Robinson's analysis.

The pervasiveness and potential significance of reading Emerson's ideas and "style" as simply artifacts of literary composition is perhaps best exemplified more recently by an exasperated, if also somewhat tongue-in-cheek, criticism of Emerson's place in the literary canon. William Major and Bryan Sinche argue in a 2010 op-ed for the *Chronicle of Higher Education* that the time has come to "give the boot" to the "cult of Ralph Waldo Emerson," a cult that insists on Emerson's significance to not only the American literary tradition but also to contemporary culture more broadly. In Emerson, Major and Sinche find a noxious optimism and validation of student narcissism, but they reserve special condemnation for Emerson's style—a condemnation that is worth discussing because it so closely resembles criticism levied against Emerson in his own time:

> Because of Emerson's obscurantist and peripatetic style, his meanings—assuming there are some—are hidden. . . .
>
> The savvy English major comes away delighted with Emerson's aphorisms and amazed by his ability to thrust together barely related concepts that seem like a viable argument. In that way, Emerson reminds us of the novitiate graduate student who attempts to write theory for the first time. Having read a little, and having been both confused and charmed by it, the student dives in, employing language and concepts barely understood. The result is predictable nonsense. Emerson, too, picks and grabs, looking for a viable path through the forest. The problem, though, is that he has landed himself in a cumbersome thicket. What

> emerges is a bloated monster that has just gorged itself on nature, God, spirit, reason, understanding, and virtue, to name just a few.

Of course, this assessment is not scholarly in any traditional sense, yet it responds in ways that hearken to those auditors of Emerson's lectures (and, for that matter, of contemporary critics of his essays) who found Emerson's speaking only, as the editorial insists, "predictable nonsense." His writing is a "bloated monster" that provide readers with the occasional, delightful aphorism.

The parallels between this assessment and, say, of Wilson Flagg, one of many of Emerson's contemporary detractors, are striking in their comments on Emerson's style. Again, the point here is not so much whether or not a particular person finds Emerson agreeable but how the commentators' responses to Emerson's method of expression reveal as much about the culture that heard him as it does about Emerson himself. For Flagg,

> the Emersonians, whether employed upon ethics or theology, never try to prove anything. When a thing is to be proved, there must be a certain relation between the sentences that make paragraphs. We cannot argue in the oracular style, though it might answer a good purpose if a lawyer was arguing a bad case before a Concord jury. If we would reason, we must take for our model among the ancients, not Epictetus or the Brahmins,—but Marcus Tullius Cicero. (bMs Am 1130.12)

Flagg's insistence on Ciceronian arrangement here bears uncanny resemblance to Major and Sinche's criticism of Emerson's essay style. Emerson and his ilk demonstrate an unwillingness to follow formal rules of argumentation; they fail to create logical relationships between sentences, or even to form a paragraph. This is, for many, Emerson's refusal to "prove anything."

That Emerson was not attempting to prove anything was apparently beyond the thinking of Flagg and those like him, and yet it illustrates precisely why Emerson, in deliberately attempting to upend such modes of delivery, should be considered especially important to American oratorical culture. For however much he may have been dismissed, and for however much his way of expressing ideas may have befuddled some listeners, he remained in high demand for nearly thirty years on the lecture circuit, fetching fees far above most other speakers. His rhetoric had an impact.

Notably, and the point for scholars who would approach Emerson as rhetorician, commentaries like those mentioned earlier often situate themselves as responses to classical argument and arrangement and identify his work as what Major and Sinche call "the prose of a crazy person." Doing so fails to imagine the historical significance of Emersonian expression in terms of oratorical culture, let alone prose writing. Much of Emerson's "prose" is actually adaptation and editorial construction of lectures, which means understanding it requires consideration of how his "style" works against prevailing modes of oral delivery as much as, if not more than, written expression. To make this point clear, one might imagine Emerson as essentially creating free verse for the podium. As Whitman's verse sought to disrupt the constraints of poetic forms, so too did Emerson for the new literature of the lecture.

An investigation of Emerson's personal and public writing and speaking reveals that he remained concerned about the nature of rhetoric throughout his life, finding it increasingly hemmed in by formalities that governed not simply expression but the ability of an audience to learn and grow. His words, accordingly, do not resemble argumentation in an Aristotelian or even belletristic way. They do not arrange themselves according to a dialectical system or slavish adherence to classical arrangement. Instead, they disrupt such structures, purposefully so. Those criticisms that fixate on Emerson's "inability" to craft logical argument, in other words, reveal as much about audience expectation as they do about his particular writing and speaking styles. Even if one finds Emerson's "bloated" prose disagreeable, any criticism along that line points directly to why Emerson is so essential to nineteenth-century American rhetoric. His style is, in fact, a deliberate confrontation with the political and material constraints of the lyceum circuit. He consciously aims to undermine form in order to make a statement about function. In the same way that William Faulkner challenged the form of the novel, or Emily Dickinson the structure of the poem, or Ludwig Wittgenstein the construction of philosophical chatter, Emerson's lectures challenge not only audience expectations but the institutional structures that control those expectations and leave listeners, as he would say of readers in "Some Good Books," "coming and going like a dog" (*LL* 2: 230).

Dehistoricizing Emerson from the lecture hall and rhetorical history leads, then, to deeply problematic readings of Emerson's work. In the case of Major and Sinche, it leads to dismissing Emerson's writing as lunacy. While such readings of Emerson are likely not unfamiliar to teachers of nineteenth-century American literature, who must help students (and colleagues) make sense of a new, and apparently unapproachable, style, one can only relegate his significance to the margins of nineteenth-century America by reading him outside the context of a deliberate attempt to disrupt institutions of public speaking, whether pulpit or podium. Indeed, Emerson's project embodies a radical spirit that continues to inform current American writing. The desire to upend traditions is a hallmark of the American literary canon, however it may be conceived, and so it is with the rhetorical tradition as well. The only reason Emerson might not be considered central to his rhetorical milieu is because he refused to participate in its conventions. He wanted to challenge those conventions, and he demanded of himself early on that his lecturing career break from prevailing modes of delivery.

Archival Research, Lecture Expectations, and Rhetorical Dissonance

Emerson's audiences came to lecture halls with specific expectations about lecture propriety that were increasingly secular, scientific, and business-oriented, and that orientation brought with it attendant lecture conventions. Archival research (which marks much of the best Emerson scholarship) has provided invaluable understandings of Emerson as a lecturer along these lines and how he was received by his audiences. Much of that research has relied on theories of reception emerging from literary or cultural studies and has helped illuminate the mixed response Emerson received when he spoke. Berlin, Bosco and Myerson, Cameron, Cayton, Charvat, Robinson, Wilchens, and any number of other commentators have discussed the polarized reviews Emerson received, and Robinson notes that this was at once the charm and the frustration of hearing Emerson speak.

Nonetheless, a richer understanding of the rhetorical history that shaped and prepared audiences for oratory helps explain precisely why Emerson's speaking garnered simultaneous praise and condemnation and, in some cases, confusion. Rhetorical culture molded auditors. They carried with them the history of oratory each time they entered a lecture hall. If orators had been trained in certain modes of delivery, audiences too had been taught to expect those modes. In much the same way that today's audiences are "trained" to expect certain features to appear when they buy a ticket for an action movie or a romance (and can be deeply disappointed and frustrated when those traits do not appear), so too did audiences in the nineteenth century recognize and expect the constituent elements of an oration and lecture.[5]

Cayton provides a useful reminder of one way these expectations may have functioned in lecture halls when she points out that in "lyceums and Mechanics' Institutes, knowledge that had formerly been defined only as religious, literary, or scientific began to be defined also as practical or pragmatic" ("Making" 79). That drift to the dissemination of practical knowledge was reflected in the increasing influence of highly stylized forms of delivery and recognizable systems of expression that governed speaking propriety in these settings. Cayton demonstrates convincingly that many audiences of Emerson, in fact, tried to extract from his orations the practical advice they often came to lectures seeking. She claims that "Emerson may have been systematically misconstrued by his audience" in that the audience took away from his lectures practical, not moral, advice (93). She shows through an examination of firsthand accounts and newspaper reviews from the Midwest that "his audience heard the warrant to be a set of already familiar, pragmatic, common-sense rules for attaining individual financial and social success" (94). In short, the crowds attending Emerson's lectures wanted one thing, but Emerson delivered quite another.

Carl Bode long ago recognized that the lyceum—as an arena of practical education and instruction in scientific apparatus—brought with it stylized forms of imparting knowledge, and while variations sometimes occurred (in the same way that contemporary genre movies may have variations), the core structures governing organization and delivery were well established when Emerson rose to fame. Audiences knew what to expect, and they assumed the speakers would essentially fall in line. Indeed, as Angela Ray's meticulous study of how the lyceum shaped the American "public" demonstrates, even the physical spaces in which lectures were delivered became standardized and replicated across the country. The buildings and rooms helped shape audience expectations just as public spaces do today (see especially 21–30, 63–111). To sit in a lecture hall was to engage in an act of collective memory and to participate in an unspoken contract between orator, space, and audience.

Emerson's violation of the rules of lyceum propriety, then, unsettled many auditors, even as it inspired others. What appeared reckless to some listeners, seemed revolutionary to others. Where some heard incoherence, others heard sublime inspiration. These responses illustrate not only issues with Emerson's voice, tone, or mode of delivery; they more usefully demonstrate how Emerson's deliberate method of lecturing disrupted entrenched social expectations for public speech. So, a reviewer of Emerson's 1841 lecture on the "Method of Nature" noted, with typical expectations of a lyceum crowd: "'It is quite likely that the oration contained a great deal of *science*; but even if it did not, no one could know the fact'" (qtd. in Charvat 19). Similarly, a reviewer of Emerson's later "Eloquence" lecture seems especially offended, drawing a telling contrast between orderly commerce and disorderly speaking:

> "Ralph Waldo Emerson's lecture on Eloquence reminded us of the way it is said vessels are built on the St. Lawrence—by the mile, and then cut off to suit orders. Mr. Emerson turns over about six sheets where he reads one, and it is of no consequence where his turning over stops." (qtd. in *LL* 1: xxv)[6]

The dissonance, grounded in expectations for financial and social advice as well as practical knowledge, illustrates how rhetorical history may provide a more useful framework for understanding his lecturing than recourse to literary theory or cultural critique divorced from rhetorical criticism. Rhetorical theory and history provide the surest footing from which to climb the mountain of Emerson's lecture manuscripts.

Violating Propriety and Emerson's Revolutionary Plan to Remake the Podium

From the late eighteenth century into the nineteenth, lecture audiences would have been exposed primarily to both neoclassical and belletristic standards of oratory, and those standards regulated forms of arrangement to embody a particular form of propriety. Some of this I discuss in previous chapters (such as chapter 4), but scholarship in nineteenth-century American rhetoric has established the way these assumptions governed oratorical culture. Gregory Clark and S. Michael Halloran argue in the introduction to their seminal collection *Oratorical Culture in Nineteenth-Century America: Transformations in the Theory and Practice of Rhetoric* that the nineteenth-century conception of rhetoric progressed from figuring the orator as civic deliberator to individualistic contemplator. They begin their discussion by acknowledging the significance of Gerald Graff's observation that oratorical culture governed college life, but they extend that claim to insist that it governed public deliberation more broadly. The early nineteenth century witnessed a "discourse drawn self-consciously on the model of classical Roman rhetoric," which "enacted the neoclassical assumption that moral authority in a community is located in the public consensus of its members rather than in their individual private convictions" (2). The early American orators, then, viewed themselves as involved in public deliberation, working with an audience to reach agreement on general principles. The goal of a speaker was to reach that consensus so that it might be applied in novel ways to particular circumstances. Clark and Halloran point out, though, that this model eventually gives way to one where the individual becomes more highly prized than the communal consensus, and as a result, orators begin to shape their work to activate individual "truths." For Clark and Halloran,

> this transformation in the motivation of rhetoric in America during the nineteenth century suggests a diminishing ability of American public culture to function collectively—for us, one of the losses. However, the emergence of these specialized communities gave access to the theory and practice of public discourse to people who had never had access before—for us, one of the gains. (6)

This vital transformation should be considered when examining Emerson's career as a lecturer. While it is likely too tidy of a narrative, it nonetheless illustrates how oratorical culture evolves throughout the century, and if we read Emerson as living through that change, we might see precisely why his frustration became increasingly pronounced. Clark and Halloran use Emerson as a foil in their discussion, drawing on literary representations of his work to figure him as ultimate purveyor of self-culture—to them, a sign of a radical turn inward that distances the speaker from the audience and communal well-being. Such a reading, however, fails to consider how deeply Emerson read in rhetorical theory and how he aimed not just for individual truth but for civic obligation as well. Such concerns I have tried to illustrate in previous chapters, but here, I draw attention to it because if that narrative were true—that Emerson was so deeply concerned with self-culture that only individual concerns mattered—we would find in him increasing satisfaction with his role in oratorical culture. The transformation from consensus to individualism would be a success, for his way of seeing the world would have triumphed over and against the communal decision-making process, and the individual mind would guide and support a culture.

While such a reading of Emerson is convenient, it misses Emerson's enduring and deepening dissatisfaction with an individualism that had no sense of the communal. It was variety without unity, diversity without harmony. For this, Emerson certainly drew from some of aspects of belletrism, but his break from them is grounded in a radical sense of how the individual fit into the collective—how the self is obliterated when a greater collective wisdom prevails. This might best be seen in Emerson's mirroring an aspect of neoclassical rhetoric that Clark and Halloran highlight as a great common good: "the insistent refusal to draw a sharp line between contemplation and action, between the academy and the public forum" (7). Emerson, as I have tried to demonstrate throughout this book, steadfastly refused to separate contemplation and action because only through the yoking of the two could a more just society emerge.

Clark and Halloran's analysis focuses on oratorical culture, but Nan Johnson, who traces the lineage of Common Sense rhetorics in the wide range of rhetorical handbooks published throughout the nineteenth century, sees similar transformations. Johnson describes the evolution of handbooks by positioning them against early British versions of them and Scottish rhetorical theory. While recent scholarship has suggested that other influences may have comparable effects, Johnson's study remains a standard in understanding how American rhetorics can best be understood as transatlantic negotiations of rhetorical theory. In her work, she draws careful distinctions between the enactment of the individual's power and the obligations to social good. She describes an increasing dependence on a "systematic architecture" imported from British New Rhetorics, one that "relied on a combination of the theoretical rationales and systematic schemes" in their development (*Nineteenth-Century Rhetoric* 65–66). These schemes led to a series of increasingly codified methods of expression, accounting for, in part, the rapid rise and popularity of the elocutionary movement, with its highly stylized forms of delivery. Further, the orator rose in importance in the American scene, becoming "an agent of edification, a delegate of culture." This role as delegate, however, brought with it significant responsibility to engage in public debate. Providing a counterstatement to Clark and Halloran on the rise of this individualized power, then, Johnson suggests that

> rhetorical practice provides the individual with an expressive voice and society with the means to dispense justice, debate policy, and exalt the beauties of truth and nature. By justifying the

> study and practice of rhetoric in these terms, the nineteenth-century rhetorical tradition corroborated one of the most earnest beliefs of nineteenth-century North American society: that the productive exchange of ideas between rational minds furthers progress of democratic society and protects the fortunes of all. (246)

In this analysis, the shifting rhetoric, though increasingly systematized, maintains a focus on the common good and public debate, even if it began to emphasize the power of the individual. The result is that "rhetoricians claimed for rhetoric the status of science, practical art, and civil servant," whereby "the mind and heart are trained to the service of the individual intellect and the social good" (*Nineteenth-Century Rhetoric* 246). The point here is that the emphasis on the self and self-culture that animates Emerson's work does not necessitate the idea that he abdicated a belief in the ability of rhetoric to shape civic discourse. Indeed, his dissatisfaction with the increasing systemization of oratorical modes is grounded on the idea that such systems are unable to help audiences gain a sense of common good. The activation of individual insight, the firing of revelation that Emerson believed to be the heart of the orator's role, is impossible in rhetorical systems in the same way that it is impossible with homiletic forms. Emerson's displeasure with the podium is substantiated by the precise frustration he felt for the limits imposed on the pulpit.

Johnson's history of American rhetorical theory focuses on these increasingly reified systems, and so predictably, Emerson appears only once in Johnson's history. He was refusing to participate in the types of systems that began to dominate, so Johnson notes his ideas only when one of the nineteenth-century handbook writers cites Emerson's explicit concern with audience: "Emerson's point that the platform speaker must possess exceptional sensitivity to audience in order to compel action is indicative of the widely held nineteenth-century view that the oratory who seeks to persuade must have a keen insight into how emotions move the will" (*Nineteenth-Century Rhetoric* 164), and yet he embodies the development and eventual loss of a specific type of rhetorical theory that worked outside the constraints of handbook systems.

Because Emerson spoke to assemblies deeply enculturated to lecture propriety (albeit perhaps unwittingly so), lecture attendees—especially those who primarily sought material gain through an individualistic focus on the self—Emerson lost hope in the power of the lyceum to transform

American culture.[7] Indeed, as Cayton has suggested, by the end of his career as a lecturer, he had lost the belief in the revolutionary nature of the lyceum gathering because of what Martin Hewitt has called public and newspaper responses to "conventional lecturing controls" (12). Even so, Emerson refused to allow his lectures to conform to cultural expectations. He saw his work as fostering genuine civic action that could have immediate power to transform an audience. His lectures sought to elevate the listener through a new rhetoric, and he uses the image of the panharmonicon to exemplify his vision.

Panharmonic, Harmony in Diversity

In an entry from Emerson's *Topical Notebook PH*, Emerson invokes an image for speaking style that may be the best emblem for his vision of lecturing: "A man's style is his Mind's voice. Wooden minds, wooden voices. Truth is shrill as a fife, various as a panharmonicon" (*TN* 2: 375). The image here is twofold, moving from fife to panharmonicon, but relying on the connection between the sound and the voice, and capturing the core feature of Emerson's rhetoric: its insistence on variety. Emerson's transcendentalism, with its sense of unity and its assertion of universal truth, tends to obfuscate the central feature of Emerson's epistemology, politics, and rhetoric—its diversity. While a grand unity may exist, Emerson repeatedly contends that the access to it comes through the wide variety of voices that utter it into the world (see chapters 1 and 2 of this study). No single one captures it. No single person can lay claim to it. Emerson's collection *Representative Men* illustrates this point well as it uses individuals to represent core features of ethical minds and action in the world. The point of that volume, like the emblem of the panharmonicon, is the necessity of variety to gain access to unity. Further, that variety is not simply stylistic but is wedded to the mind of the person speaking.

The panharmonicon was the invention of Johann Maelzel, a German who is credited with creating, among other musical automatons, the metronome in 1814. Maelzel debuted the panharmonicon in 1804, and it was imagined as a kind of orchestra in a box. Effectively a pipe organ with percussion elements, the mechanism could imitate the sounds of any instrument in an orchestra and created a notoriously haunting set of harmonies (Partridge). The invention was the first automated playing machine, and some years later Maelzel would design a machine that, when connected to a piano, could accurately produce a written version of the music being played. Beethoven wrote his 1813 *Battle Symphony* for the panharmonicon, and according to Carmel Raz, the instrument shaped Honoré de Balzac's ruminations on medical treatments for nervous disorders. In 1811, a panharmonicon was brought to Boston, but in 1826 Maelzel apparently brought a new one with him on his visit to the United States (Maelzel and Jones 132). On that visit, rumors circulated that he had sold the automatic music maker for the princely (and impossible-to-believe) sum of four hundred thousand dollars (Hale 603). During that trip, he exhibited the machine and others—including the "Chess Player, the Austrian Trumpeter, and the Rope Dancers"—in April 1826 to a crowd of about one hundred people (Fiske 430). Maelzel was apparently no great showman, and his chess machine in particular took special hits in the press, but he was well received and well liked. According to Daniel Fiske,

> his appearance and manners attracted the applause of his visitors. He was the perfection of politeness and amiability; he was passionately fond of children, and invariably reserved for them his front seats and distributed sweetmeats among them; and he occasionally gave a benefit to orphans, or widows, or some other charity, in a way that evinced real benevolence of disposition. (432)

After 1826, Maelzel returned to the United States twice more (in 1828 and 1833), during which time Emerson must have witnessed the panharmonicon's magic. In an August 1834 journal entry, he reflects on the idea of freedom, noting that "a very small part of a man's voluntary acts are such as agree perfectly with his conviction," and he wonders whether, as each person goes about his day unconscious of the "incongruity" between his actions and innermost thoughts, it really matters what animates the action if it still represents the man: "The man might as well be gone, so he leave a Maelzel machine in his place" (*JMN* 4: 312).

The ability of the automaton to replicate the sounds of virtually any orchestral instrument captured Emerson's imagination, and it provided him with a compelling image for describing the variety that, working together, sounds the truth. Indeed, a "Maelzel machine" could apparently do more than simply imitate; it could, he hoped, actually replace the original. It represents, then, an organ of democratic expression, and it perfectly embodies what Emerson desires the orator to do. It harmonizes all.

Emerson invokes the image of the panharmonicon more than once to describe the power of the lecture, including, besides those already indicated earlier, an entry that demonstrates the depth of hope Emerson had for the capacity for the lecture as a form of expression to foster change:

> I look on the Lecture Room as the true Church of the coming time, and as home of a richer eloquence than Faneuil Hall or the Capitol ever knew. For here is all that the true orator will ask, namely, a convertible audience,—an audience coming up to the house, not knowing what shall befall them there, but uncommitted and willing victims to reason and love. There is no topic that may not be treated, and no method excluded. *Here*, everything is admissible, philosophy, ethics, divinity, criticism, poetry, humor, anecdote, mimicry,—ventriloquism almost,—all the breadth and versatility of the most liberal conversation, and of the highest, lowest, personal, and local topics—all are permitted, and all may be combined in one speech. It is a panharmonicon combining every note on the longest gamut, from the explosion of cannon to the tinkle of a guitar.
>
> . . . Here is a pulpit that makes the other chairs of instruction cold and ineffectual with their customary preparation for a delivery: the most decorous with fine things, pretty things, wise things, but no arrows, no axes, no nectar, no transpiercing, no loving, no enchantment. Here, the American orator shall find the theatre he needs; here, he may lay himself out utterly large, prodigal, enormous, on the subject of the hour. Here, he may dare to hope for the higher inspiration and a total transfusion of himself into the minds of men. (*LL* 1: 48)[8]

The rapturous quality of Emerson's description (and I quote it at length in part because of its breathlessness) demonstrates a degree of hope that Emerson usually reserves for the closing of his own lectures. It exhorts, even as it catalogues the reasons and possibilities for the lecture's ability to change an audience. At the heart of that ability—the key aspect of it—is the idea that a lecture can cast aside the "decorous" and "customary preparation for a delivery" because in the lecture hall, "everything is admissible . . . all are permitted, and all may be combined in one speech." The lecture is a panharmonicon that makes every sound, from a cannon blast to a guitar strum, part of its surprise performance for the one thing that "the true orator" most desires: "a convertible audience." The sheer variety, which allows the performance a remarkable diversity of sounds, topics, and opinions, ensures that the lecture hall becomes the place for "higher inspiration."[9]

This emphasis on variety—on rejection of "method"—explains why Emerson, so often ridiculed or disparaged for his speaking style, also found his admirers. Nancy Craig Simmons's reception studies of Emerson's speeches is particularly important in this regard. Her work demonstrates the breadth of responses to Emerson when he lectured, suggesting that Emerson's message may have been better understood than once thought. She notes that Cayton's assessment that the audience members usually misunderstood Emerson as enforcing their own cultural standards, not challenging them, might be misleading, at least with the New England series.

Simmons, nevertheless, raises an important question that returns in spirit to some of Cayton's analysis: why was Emerson dissatisfied with the newspaper coverage of his New England series? Why did he feel misunderstood? Simmons answers these questions by looking at the content of Emerson's speeches, concluding that, in fact, most of the reports of this time were not misunderstandings of content, and thus perhaps not so far off the mark as Emerson might have believed. Perhaps, Simmons implies, Emerson's dissatisfaction was misplaced.

Emerson's displeasure with newspaper reporting, however, concerned not only the content of the speeches (such as how they were summarized) but also with form (in other words, how they were delivered). Emerson's lectures are not simply about ideas; they also embody revolutionary thinking, an exploration of lecture form that might awaken those passive souls in his audiences and move them to action. James Crosswhite, in discussing Emerson's resistance to speaking about "'public questions,'" imagines Emerson as engaged in an act of cultural resistance, not because he did not care but because he did not accept the terms of the argument. Crosswhite suggests that Emerson can best be read as conveying the idea that

> I cannot confine myself to speaking within the acknowledged semiotic codes of my time, within the accepted ideologies, or discourses. There is not only a prison or slavery acknowledged within these ideologies, including the ideology of abolitionism, but there is a deeper slavery and imprisonment, in the ideologies that keep us in the business of slavery and imprisonment regardless of who is enslaved or in jail at the time. (79–80)

Crosswhite, here, might be faulted for imagining Emerson's resistance to cultural strictures as the privilege of someone in a position of power, but figuring Emerson as essentially refusing to participate in the genres of expression that made "slavery and imprisonment" possible astutely depicts Emerson's project. It also explains his audiences' frustration and, for that matter, his own frustration in trying to achieve a "true" eloquence.

Certainly, a listener might understand what Emerson had to say in general, but did his words spark the fire, generate the heat, he so much wished to inspire? If they did not, Emerson's project would have failed—in his own mind anyway. If he had gained assent but had not changed entire ways of being in the world by challenging the assumptions of what could be done in the podium, then his project was just intellectual mimicry. He wanted more than that. He wanted irresistible truth, and he believed it would only happen through shattering the forms that constrained the diverse modes of speaking that might otherwise inspire action.

The newspaper reports that Simmons cites demonstrate that journalists repeatedly labelled Emerson's lectures in stereotypically belletristic language, evaluating them in terms that reinforced deeply entrenched cultural conventions. The journalists describe Emerson as having "vigorous common sense" (53), "elegance" and "force" (53), "freshness of thought" and "boldness of judgment" (54), and "melody of diction" (71). None of these terms are arbitrary; they are keywords of American belletristic oratory, and in some cases neoclassical theory; they represent traits espoused by the New Rhetorics of the eighteenth century. So, if we understand Emerson as wanting to offer a new oratory, a new ideal orator, as he would a new ideal American poet, we must remember that part of that uniqueness comes from a new style to reflect the new lecture. It should be organic, purposefully nonsystematic and, perhaps, devoid of all those belletristic traits that Emerson was working hard to undo. It should represent an almost impossible range of sounds, capturing the diversity of experience in the same way that the panharmonicon replicates a range of music impossible through any other instrument. In other words, Emerson was disappointed by being reviewed as just another American orator, recapitulating the same traditions, sounds, and conventions of the New Rhetorics, and I suspect that in our failure to really grapple with how Emerson fits in his rhetorical moment, we have replicated the failures of his contemporary press. We have failed to see his attempt to usher in a new rhetorical era, one more expansive than any other before.

The word *ambition* is rarely discussed in Emersonian circles, and yet Emerson's deliberate attempt to theorize a new rhetoric, a new poetics, and even a new country was remarkably ambitious. He would never claim himself a prophet or a leader of a movement in the way that some of his intellectual disciples would, but that does not minimize the capacity he believed he (and anyone else for that matter) possessed to enact meaningful and far-reaching change in American culture. He wanted to revolutionize how Americans acted in the world. He wanted to unshackle them and foster new challenges to old traditions. He didn't aim simply to rock a boat or two; he intended to capsize ships. Frigates and steamers at that, carrying payloads of cultural treasures that most believed priceless and irreplaceable. And yet we eschew the word *ambition* despite the fact that it best represents Emerson's goal, which was to usher in for the first time "a nation of men" (*CW* 1: 70).

Emerson saw clearly that public action was the only way that could happen, and his rhetorical theory and mode of oratory should be read as one of multiple attempts across different genres to give that vision voice and public expression. Emerson's lecturing embodied his belief that new methods of public discourse would encourage others to experience the world in a new way, and his rhetoric was the foundation on which he built not only a career but also a vision for reconciling the life of the mind with public action, ideas with civic virtue. As such, Emerson's rhetorical theory embodies a democratic tradition grounded on idealism and insistence on civic responsibility. His lecture style, expansive and panharmonic, ultimately represents, then, a vein of rhetoric that has been lost to one of the things he feared most: endless systemization of knowledge and unchallenged adoption of traditions. Recovery of similar histories of rhetoric can only occur when our own definitions of what constitutes "theory" expand to include those who sensed the limiting qualities of the dominant modes of speaking. When that shift occurs, the wide range of expression in a democratic culture will begin to enliven our discussion not only of the forms of rhetoric but the challenging ideas that animate them as well. We will hear the sounds of instruments that have been lost despite their revolutionary, even breathless, beauty and possibilities. Perhaps, we will find the one thing Emerson so desperately sought: a grand unity that somehow never marginalizes, never silences.

CONCLUSION

Distilling Emerson's Rhetorical Theory and Prospects for Future Study

This study has had two primary goals. First, it has aimed to persuade rhetoric scholars that Emerson deserves more than passing reference in the history of rhetoric and in our considerations of American rhetorical theory. Second, it has aspired to persuade literary scholars that in order to secure Bosco and Myerson's "full accounting" of Emerson as a lecturer and language theorist, a nuanced understanding of rhetorical history and theory is needed. Achieving these two goals requires cross-disciplinary talk and collaboration, and it likely obliges us to rethink some of our fundamental assumptions about Emerson's America.

I've tried to make it clear throughout this study that such an approach is not a wholesale repudiation of other approaches. Indeed, it is grounded on many of them. For example, the careful manuscript research of Emerson scholars makes a study like this one possible. I have, throughout this work, relied on literary scholars' archival research because generations of those scholars have assiduously recovered and made public reams of Emerson family manuscripts that would otherwise have been forgotten. Those scholars have engaged in a decades' long process of reorienting us to Emerson and his times, and they have produced what may be the most detailed and thorough accounting of a nineteenth-century author's life and work that exists. Indeed, that project is still ongoing, and further discoveries will undoubtedly follow that will change how we think about Emerson as a rhetorician.

Historians of rhetoric should be encouraged to know that because their literary peers have maintained a steadfast program of manuscript research, rich opportunities for Emerson scholarship exist. While rhetoricians have, since early speech communication scholars first discussed

Emerson's rhetoric, acknowledged his significance, the depth of that engagement has slowly accelerated over the last twenty years. That is thanks in large part to the publication of a range of Emerson's primary texts that had long been unpublished, but it is also thanks to rhetoricians who, since Berlin, have had a sneaking suspicion that Emerson may be more important than what we once thought. What most will discover, I think, is that failure to examine Emerson as a rhetorical theorist results in a glaring omission from American rhetorical history and, indeed, rhetorical history more broadly.

I suggest that the impact extends beyond American rhetorical history because as Emerson's relevance to rhetorical studies has inched toward greater recognition, so too has his debt to a wide range of international writers, poets, and speakers. Emerson studies have taken a decidedly international turn recently, with compelling work suggesting Emerson's deep engagement with figures as diverse as Confucius and Hafez (referred to as Hafiz in Emerson's time) (LaRocca and Miguel-Alfonso). Such work, as I will discuss further in this chapter, promises to direct us to the subtle influence of foreign rhetorics on American idealism. With that, we will undoubtedly find promising new correspondences that will illuminate the revolutionary quality of Emerson's rhetorical theory.

Distilling the Traits of an Emersonian Rhetoric

This study has focused almost exclusively on theories that derive from widely acknowledged, seminal rhetorical texts. As Emerson began to conceive of himself as a lecturer, he sought out those written documents that describe the role of the orator, the ethics of persuasion, and the connection between the self, the spirit, and language. His voluminous readings in rhetoric illustrate a man who might be seen as obsessed with the topic if his extensive readings in so many other topics did not suggest that he simply was an engaged intellectual across many fields. Still, rhetoric was no passing interest for Emerson. Instead, it remained a lifelong fascination that he nurtured through historical readings from what we now call the rhetorical tradition.

Of course, Emerson frequently had doubts about traditions, so we should not be surprised that he frequently conceived of his own rhetoric as a corrective to the work of his forebears. The chapters of this study have attempted to demonstrate precisely what Emerson borrowed and what he rejected from those theorists as he sought to both define and embody an American rhetoric. He insisted on several key qualities for rhetoric, which form the foundation of an Emersonian rhetorical theory.

First, Emerson devoted himself to the idea of a "true rhetoric." He explicitly invoked Plato's question for a transcendental rhetoric, but his development of the idea is decidedly more democratic and expansive than Plato's. Nonetheless, Emerson, like Plato and Augustine, insisted that rhetoric aim for transcendence. "Mere persuasion" was noxious to him, and the idea that both an orator and an auditor might experience the divine through a shared process of communication was palpable to him. He yearned to "take sovereign possession" of his audience, even as he believed that to do so he must resign himself to a universal, shared power that animated both himself and his listeners.

Second, Emerson decried systemization and undue formality and emphasized imagination. Indeed, the heart of his belief that language could change minds was founded on the idea that rhetoric, in its truest form, upends tradition and ushers something new into the world. His valorization of the language of the streets—even to the point of embracing the vulgar—is best understood as part of his resistance to traditional rhetorical forms. Emerson's linking of Cicero and Burke is the clearest example of how he negotiates the problematic relationship between common language and sublime nobility, but even his repudiation of American misappropriations of belletrism demonstrates that for him, a system was simply reified dogmatism. The faculty of the imagination destroys dogmatism, and a true rhetoric breaks things apart. It fractures landscapes and sweeps away unnecessary forms. All that is left is the churning, roiling truth breaking through in unpredictable (if not inexplicable) ways.

As such, and Emerson's third, and perhaps most revolutionary, quality of rhetoric is that it is panharmonic. Emerson argues that true rhetoric is more than simply democratic accessibility to the means of persuasion. He is not particularly interested in access to formal education in rhetoric, and though he more than once touts the idea that any person can hurl an eloquent phrase from time to time, his emphasis on democratic expression extends far beyond one person's ability to be eloquent at any particular moment. For Emerson, the most essential aspect of rhetorical exchange was that varied expressions harmonize only when each is honored as offering a truth to be heard. In other words, rhetoric is not simply just accessible to all but through a radically expansive and inclusive set of voices moves an audience toward truth and reconciliation with divinity.

By analogy, the sounds of the forest may be dominated by the shrill call of the hawk, but the forest can only be understood when the chirping of the sparrow, the scurrying of the mouse in the leaves, the wisp of wind through the pines, and the cracking of the woodpecker on a tree trunk come together to provide a full picture of the scene.[1] The rhetor's job is, to be sure, to make his own noise, but it is also to recognize that his sounds are meaningless without the sounds of others. He joins a chorus, and in that harmony, truth emerges.

The search for a transcendental rhetoric, the rejection of formal systems, and the embrace of panharmony are the heart of Emerson's rhetoric, and these qualities emerge from his interaction with rhetorical theorists that he read. They derive from his lifelong exploration of rhetorical theory, and his published writings and his private journals and letters demonstrate the ongoing negotiation of rhetoric as an object of study. The point of this monograph has been to tell the story of his explicit engagement with these texts so that his place in rhetorical history is better understood within the intellectual tradition that gave it birth.

There are, however, other stories worth telling, so I conclude this study by pointing to some of the more important ones that fall outside the aims of this particular text. My hope is that this study prompts greater engagement with Emerson as a rhetorical theorist. Placing him alongside prominent figures in (the admittedly unsettled) canon of rhetorical history provides a useful way of telling Emerson's story, but other approaches will lead to new stories, particularly those that connect him to his contemporaries who, like him, were struggling with a rapidly shifting American rhetorical culture. While not an exhaustive list, the prospects given represent some of the most compelling stories yet to be fully told about Emerson and his relationship to rhetorical culture.

CONFLICTED NINETEENTH-CENTURY RHETORICS

For many years, nineteenth-century American rhetorical theory was seen as hardly more than an adaptation of belletrism to the American scene. That view has come under considerable scrutiny as an increasing number of scholars look beyond the belletristic tradition and the many replications of Blair's work in American rhetoric textbooks. Four especially noteworthy developments will help us better contextualize and rethink Emerson's contributions.

First, the expansion of the canon of rhetorical theory to include women has fundamentally changed the idea of the "rhetorical tradition." Much of this was sparked with the publication of Andrea Lunsford's *Reclaiming Rhetorica* and Cheryl Glenn's *Rhetoric Retold*, the former a collection of essays that sought to demonstrate that the exclusion of the feminine from rhetorical studies represented not only an intellectual injustice but also a fundamentally flawed historical project. Included in the collection is an examination of one of Emerson's great colleagues, Margaret Fuller. Fuller's impact on Emerson continues to garner significant scholarly attention, but her influence on Emerson's thinking on rhetoric is far from complete, and her writings may require us to rethink American rhetorical theory.

Fuller self-consciously fashioned a mode of delivery based on the idea of conversation, and she emphasized the dialogic quality of human expression. Emerson writes at length about "conversation" and interpersonal communication, and the relationship between Fuller and Emerson on this count surely requires further study. For example, in his rarely given lecture "Table Talk," Emerson provides an extended discussion of conversation's value as a rhetoric. Predictably, Emerson intermixes industrial and natural metaphors to assert its value: "I prize the mechanics of conversation. 'Tis pulley, and lever, and screw. To fairly disengage the mass, and send it gingling down, a good boulder,—a block of quartz and gold,—to be worked up at leisure in the useful arts of life,—is a wonderful relief" (*LL* 2: 363). Conversation here functions to mine the deepest of ideas and make them accessible for refining. Indeed, as he says a few paragraphs later, "strict discourse with a friend is the magazine out of which all good writing is drawn," a sentiment that points to a relationship between oral and written discourse that is tantalizing in its possibilities for study. Emerson even finds in conversation a grounding in a relationship between ethos, reflection, and kairos. He suggests that "conversation too has its ethics of prudence and morals. It requires a quiet but firm self-control,—a control which now holds the subject of discourse, now lets it go, with a respect to the emergences of the moment" (*LL* 2: 364). Surrounding all this discussion of conversation, Emerson intersperses ruminations on the power of speech and the role of "sublime oratory" in society. He ultimately figures the art of conversation as having a special, persistent power:

> Conversation, when it is best, is a series of intoxications. Not Aristotle, not Kant or Hegel, but conversation is the right metaphysical professor. This is the true school of philosophy, the

> college where you learn what Thoughts are: What powers lurk in those fugitive gleams, and what becomes of them; how they make history. . . . For, in discourse with a friend, our thought, hitherto wrapped in our consciousness, detaches itself, and allows itself to be seen as a thought, in a manner as new and entertaining to us, as to our companions. (*LL* 2: 365)

This summative passage imagines conversation as the birthing of ideas into the world. Formerly locked away in our minds, conversation calls ideas forth and makes them public. Importantly, those thoughts, now spoken into the world, represent new, intoxicating metaphysics.

Jane Donawerth's *Conversational Rhetoric*, which extends her feminist rhetorical tradition outlined in "Transforming the History of Rhetorical Theory" years before, demonstrates rather convincingly that conversation rhetoric constitutes a tradition in its own right. Of course, Emerson might be seen as particularly patriarchal or aristocratic, but given his admiration for Fuller, such a reading likely understates the revolutionary quality that Emerson believed conversation possessed. Recent research on parlor rhetoric, conduct manuals, and rhetorical space, especially work by Susan Miller, Roxanne Mountford, and Nan Johnson, may provide a framework for inquiring into the nature of Fuller's "conversations," even as it may indicate a subversive rhetoric that worked within very specific cultural constraints. Such work has built on Patricia Bizzell's now widely cited call "to look in places not previously studied for work by women that would not have been traditionally considered rhetoric" (51), and it bears uncanny resemblance to the feminist turn in studies of transcendentalism that have recovered the impact of women on the movement. Phyllis Cole, Christina Zwarg, Sarah Wider, and others have mined nineteenth-century manuscripts to demonstrate that, just as rhetorical theory may be so deeply gendered as to ignore contributions by women, so too have the traditional inquiries into American romanticism failed to account for pervasive contributions by women.

Further, rhetoric scholars such as Shirley Wilson Logan, Jacqueline Jones Royster, and Vorris Nunley, as well as religious scholars like Henry Mitchell, have demonstrated convincingly that discussion of nineteenth-century rhetoric that excludes people of color fundamentally misrepresents the diversity of expression that shaped American culture. Ongoing inquiry into the very nature of rhetoric itself challenges our notion that rhetorical theory can best be understood as the type of textually grounded, Aristotelian system that has typically dominated examination of rhetorics. Drawing on cultural histories, researchers such as Elaine Richardson and Ronald Jackson II have recovered traditions that had been entirely erased from textbooks.

Native American traditions have similarly been recovered. Ernest Stromberg has advanced a project to examine hitherto ignored representations of Native American rhetorical practices. These practices circulated outside native communities and informed the more codified rhetorical traditions that were deployed in antebellum America. As William M. Clements points out, native oratorical strategies were appropriated by prominent white orators even as those orators argued that Native American strategies reflected a "weakness of Native American intellects, especially as they revealed their poverty of language" (15). (See chapters 1 and 3 in Clements's work as well.)

These former absences to rhetorical history now serve as promising heuristics for understanding nineteenth-century rhetorics, including Emerson's. They also point to a final scholarly development surrounding conflicted antebellum rhetorics, which is the vast scholarly output concerning print culture in the late eighteenth and early nineteenth centuries. The examination of literacy and print culture provides fertile ground for scholars interested in the relationship between Emerson, diverse rhetorical traditions, oratory, and eloquence. Emerson's vast production of written texts function, in part, as an archive of nineteenth-century thinking and rhetorical expression, and as such, they contain within them the residue of a variety of rhetorical strategies that he appropriated, wittingly or not. For example, Phyllis Cole's work shows definitively that Emerson borrowed extensively from the personal (if at times pseudo-public) journals of his aunt Mary Moody Emerson, and Cole traces core tenets of transcendentalism to Mary Moody. She illustrates, in short, a shared literacy. Understanding that relationship changes our understanding of not only the roots of transcendentalism but also the landscape of publication that resulted in Mary Moody's influence having been lost even as Emerson's public stature grew. What other rhetorical traditions—hush harbor rhetoric, parlor conversations, Native American orations—emerge in Emerson's writings? When those rhetorics are recovered, not only can we more fully understand Emerson's role in public culture but we can also finally recognize the historical contingencies that made his ascension possible. We can, in other words, at last contextualize

Emerson more accurately in order to ensure he is figured as only one of many important voices of the time.

THE TRANSATLANTIC AND GLOBAL EMERSON

Emerson's debt to European intellectual and literary traditions has been a preoccupation of researchers across many disciplines. Emerson traveled throughout Europe and the British Isles, and he maintained ongoing correspondence with some of the central figures of his times. His relationship with Carlyle has been the subject of many studies, as has his relationship to the English Romantics and German transcendental philosophy, with Kantian metaphysics standing as a centerpiece of many early scholarly investigations. More recently, Nietzsche's reliance on Emerson's work in formulating his particular brand of existentialism has come to represent evidence of Emerson's significance to the history of philosophy, even as scholars have long described Emerson's debt to Locke, Hume, the ancient Greeks, and the Neo-Platonists. His travels to Italy—and his close relationship to Margaret Fuller, who would achieve national fame for her coverage of the Italian Revolution—suggest a vein of continental thinking that threads throughout his journals and essays, and his admiration for the metaphysical poets emerges with force in much of his own poetry. In all, literature and philosophy specialists have frequently represented Emerson as heir to and progenitor of certain traditions across the Atlantic, and his rhetoric demonstrates similar correspondences.

Portions of this book have tackled Emerson's debt to English and Scottish rhetorical traditions. Scottish Common Sense shaped Emerson's early learning about rhetoric, but it continued to be a touchstone throughout his career, often as a foil to a romantic rhetoric. Further, Emerson turned to Burke as a model for a new American rhetoric, and though Burke's standing within the rhetorical tradition has only recently begun to be discussed, he nonetheless figures throughout Emerson's works as an important representative of a certain type of eloquence. Other British and continental rhetorical theories undoubtedly shaped Emerson, and those lineages have yet to receive full consideration.

Emerson's debt to a wider range of international writers, poets, and thinkers, however, may provide some of the most exciting avenues of inquiry. Frederic Ives Carpenter long ago recognized the influence of Asia on Emersonian thought (as did, for that matter, many of Emerson's own contemporaries), but over the last decade, Emerson studies have turned increasingly to the relationship between Emerson and non-Western literature and philosophy. Neal Dolan and Laura Jane Wey have traced the historical connections between Emerson and China and interestingly point out a surge—on the order of more than two hundred publications—of interest in China today. The recent work of Nan Z. Da goes so far as to suggest that Emerson's reading of Chinese literature provided a foundation for his "lifelong endorsement of Universal intellectual socialism," as is stated in Da's abstract, and Alan Hodder insists that "no one [in American belles-lettres] did more to foster a sympathetic interest in classical Asian cultures than Emerson himself, along with, of course, a few of his closest Transcendentalist friends" ("Asia" 41). Hodder, for that matter, has also illuminated Emerson's connections to India, where a similar lively reemergence of scholarship has occurred. Additionally, Jeffrey Einboden has recovered the relationship between Emerson and Persian poetry, and Farhang Jahanpour has argued that the rise of transcendentalism mirrors the rise of Sufism in Persia, noting Emerson's frequently cited translation of over seven hundred lines of Hafez. Mike Unher and Sara Bano have taken that correspondence to reflect a vein of "universal tolerance" that transcendentalism shares with Sufism. Further, Emerson's allure to Egypt, a common American fascination, has not escaped notice, even if his travel there late in life remains somewhat of a mystery. In addition, Emerson's connection to Japan has yielded considerable results.

A similar turn has occurred in rhetorical studies. A surge of scholarship in Chinese, Middle Eastern, and African rhetoric began in the 1990s and has continued even as other non-Western rhetorics have garnered scholarly attention. Numerous conferences have focused on this emerging field, and the number of publications is staggering. Taken together, these parallel developments across literary and rhetorical studies suggest that Emerson may represent a focal point for the importation of new ideas about rhetoric from less widely recognized corners of the globe. The transcendentalists, broadly considered, were captivated by the literature of distant lands, and while that undoubtedly reflects the orientalism and lingering colonial instinct toward appropriation that Edward Said described, the fact that they were also engaged in extensive translation projects points to other possibilities as well. Their translations may be some of the first appearances in America of rhetorics that are only now being given serious consideration. If so, the transcendentalists may represent some of the earliest global rhetoricians.

RHETORIC AND POETICS

Emerson uses "rhetoric," "eloquence," "poetry," and "the poetic" virtually interchangeably throughout his work. For example, in his late essay on "Poetry and Imagination," he places the two modes of expression side by side as part of the same transcendent instinct. In one instance, under a subheading called "Transcendency," he suggests that the desire for divine influence permeates a population, and it is characterized by, among other things, a yearning for eloquence and poetry:

> In the dance of God there is not one of the chorus but can and will begin to spin, monumental as he now looks, whenever the music and figure reach his place and duty. O celestial Bacchus! drive them mad,—this multitude of vagabonds, hungry for eloquence, hungry for poetry, starving for symbols, perishing for want of electricity to vitalize this too much pasture, and in the long delay indemnifying themselves with the false wine of alcohol, of politics or of money. (*CW* 8: 39–40)

Later, he extends this relationship, applying a central concept of oratory to poetry:

> 'Tis a rule in eloquence, that the moment the orator loses command of his audience, the audience commands him. So, in poetry, the master rushes to deliver his thought, and the words and images fly to him to express it; whilst colder moods are forced to respect the ways of saying it, and insinuate, or, as it were, muffle the fact, to suit the poverty or caprice of their expression, so that they only hint the matter, or allude to it, being unable to fuse and mould their words and images to fluid obedience. . . .
>
> All writings must be in a degree exoteric, written to a human *should* or *would*, instead of to the fatal *is*: this holds even of the bravest and sincerest writers. (*CW* 8: 15–16)

He finds in both rhetoric and poetry not simply hope for aesthetic beauty but also an ethical prerogative, the "*should* or *would*" of human behavior. The desire for cultural revolution is latent in such exhortation, and it rests on a fundamental wedding of language to some sense of the divine. While Emerson certainly maintains a distinction between the two types of expression, he nonetheless holds that both derive from a shared instinct that can change a society.

The complicated relationship between rhetoric and poetics faded as the disciplines of rhetoric and literature became increasingly sequestered from each other. While certain thinkers, especially in cultural theory or hermeneutics, periodically explore that relationship, it nonetheless remains a largely ignored—or at the very least marginal—subject. This despite long histories of theorists and philosophers trying to make sense of how the two fields should be viewed in relation to each other. While any number of figures in nineteenth-century America, Britain, and continental Europe offer compelling starting points for renewed investigations of the topic (Carlyle, Blair, Walter Pater, Alexander Jamieson, John Seely Hart, and even Herman Melville and Harriet Beecher Stowe all come to mind), Emerson—because of his extensive writing on both topics, his prominence to both fields during his lifetime, and the longevity of his career as a lecturer, poet, and philosopher—represents an especially seductive possibility for inquiry. Indeed, as I've suggested in various places throughout this study, I think he may represent a useful lever with which to pry into some of the reasons these two domains became so deeply severed from each other.

Early versions of Emerson's essays begin with poems composed on the topic under investigation. For his two published "Eloquence" essays, the opening verse set the tone each would convey. In the first, nature metaphors suggest the subtle flow of persuasion:

> Yet before the listener's eye
> Swims the world in ecstasy,
> The forest waves, the morning breaks,
> The pastures sleep, ripple the lakes,
> Leaves twinkle, flowers like persons be,
> And life pulsates in rock or tree. (*W* 7: 59)

The ecstatic revelry here reflects Emerson's belief that true rhetoric moved audiences to revelation. He held the same belief of poetry, yoking it to the imagination's capacity for prophecy. In the poem preceding the second "Eloquence" essay, Emerson turns to more violent imagery, reflecting the fire imagery he uses throughout the essay itself:

> Self-centred; when he launched the genuine word
> It shook or captivated all who heard,
> Ran from his mouth to mountains and the sea,
> And burned in noble hearts proverb and prophecy.
> (*W* 8: 109)

As chapter 4 suggests, the prophetic fire is Emerson's wrestling with the relationship between language and action, persuasion and the drift toward truth, especially in the years surrounding the Civil War. That path was, at times, a violent, shaking path, and all the more powerful because it threatened to upend noxious cultural institutions.

Emerson's reliance on poetry to convey rhetorical power bears examination. Emerson, for example, composes poetry that surveys the eloquence of others, such as William Channing's oratory or the oratory leading into the Revolutionary War. Discussion of that poetry would benefit from more than simple historical reportage or the formation of a literary aesthetic. The poems point to Emerson's yoking of rhetoric, poetry, and ethics, his demand for the "human *should* or *would*," and his ongoing fascination with language's power to persuade. Further, they embody Emerson's belief, as examined earlier in this study, that language is action itself.

Emerson, then, provides a particularly compelling case for understanding how nineteenth-century culture struggled with the relationship between eloquence, poetry, oratory, and social action. His career as both orator and poet suggests that he bridged a divide, one that he was either consciously addressing or that was at his time no divide at all and thus latent in the work. Understanding the historical nature of what we now see as a fundamental split in disciplines may force us to rethink Emerson's poetic and rhetorical production. Even if Emerson does not represent an avenue to bring poetics and rhetoric closer together, he nonetheless illuminates the nature of the schism and the benefits and drawbacks of it. Given his emphasis on the idea of "unity in variety," Emerson's theories may help us honor diverse modes of expression without sacrificing the hope for a more coherent, inclusive humanism.

WRITING STUDIES, COMPOSITION, AND INSTITUTIONAL POWER

Emerson's prose is rarely imagined as a writing model for students. Given the types of writing demanded by our educational institutions, it never will be. Yet Emerson's rhetorical theory provides gripping ideas for writing pedagogy and for rethinking the role of writing studies in the university. In particular, Emerson's metaphor of the panharmonicon points to an especially useful ethical approach to writing pedagogy.

Writing studies, broadly considered, continues to grapple with the epistemological and ethical nature of its own discipline, with especially notable revolutions occurring since the 1970s. As process orientation overcame the limits of product-oriented writing theory in the late 1970s and 1980s, a parallel recognition of diverse methods of composition and expression emerged. Practioner-scholars like Janet Emig, Peter Elbow, and Donald Murray essentially ushered in an era that, though under considerable tension now, nonetheless fundamentally broadened our notions of what it meant to be a writer and speaker. Advocacy for "post-process" pedagogy by scholars such as Gary Olson and Joseph Petraglia expands acceptance to possible diversities of expression even further. Indeed, at the heart of most post-process theory is the idea that as process pedagogy became entrenched, it reflected a series of generalizations about the nature of "the writer" that evidence simply would not bear out as generalizable. The result is that "we have better questions now, and the notion of process no longer counts as much of an insight" (Petraglia 53), in part because those questions require us to address various literacies in the classroom and the university.

Educators from a wide range of fields—from Writing across the Curriculum, to Writing in the Disciplines, to African American studies, to linguistics, to professional and technical writing, to creative writing—have struggled to effectively justify greater inclusion in the face of institutional accountability for "academic writing."[2] Writing program administrators, as Sharon James McGee and Carolyn Handa and many others have demonstrated, consistently find themselves needing to justify their methods in order to placate administrative expectations about what constitutes "good writing." Those demands on writing pedagogy reflect fundamental institutional disagreements about the nature of writing, the purpose of writing, and the ends of writing. They are, essentially, epistemological conflicts as various stakeholders within an institution vie for control over literacy and literacy assessment.

While I would not propose that Emerson's rhetoric is a panacea for such conflicts—indeed, Emerson may well have been horrified at the direction of some of the debates—I would argue that among its more useful traits is its insistence that diverse modes of expression represent the growth—not the disintegration—of a more ethical, inclusive, and accurate accounting of the world. To enact such a theory within an institution would not require abandoning community standards for acceptable writing outcomes, but it would require that the creation of those standards be done in a more radically inclusive, broad-based, and diverse way. In other words, Emerson's notion of panharmony asks us to make more room at the table to ensure a wider range of ideas are voiced. To do so requires rhetoricians to acknowledge that their specific expertise, no matter how formidable, are in fact only one of many and to reimagine their role not so much as "final word" experts, but as advocates for greater cross-disciplinary engagement with rhetorics even while articulating the necessity of their voice in ensuring a richer, deeper harmony.

Given the contested nature of rhetoric and writing programs in so many institutions, such an approach undoubtedly sounds Pollyanna or naively idealistic. And yet the history of institutional conflict over writing instruction suggests that some approaches have yet to yield the results the field has so long hoped for. Turning to a new ethical grounding, one that emphasizes inclusion as an institutional practice, requires leadership from community members uniquely qualified to analyze, communicate, and persuade. It requires writing as a discipline to abandon the rhetoric on which the discipline continues to draw strength and solidarity: a rhetoric of the outcast and misunderstood community member. It requires a sense of disciplinary identity that appreciates the necessity of its own voice without overvaluing it, driven by the "courage to ask questions, Courage to expose our ignorance" (*LL* 2: 371).

Emerson inevitably moves readers toward idealism, but he also points to the difficulty of actualizing it. Rethinking the foundations of our key cultural institutions, let alone rhetoric's place within them, is a tall order, but it is one that Emerson explicitly calls for in his persistent pleas for revolution. Late in his life, he often directed his pleas to purveyors of what he called "a commercial education":

> But I, Gentlemen, wish to see the college put on quite another foundation. I wish the college not to make you rich or great; No, but the reverse: The college is to show you the riches of the poor; to shame the vain; to show you that the common daylight is worth something; to show you that the material pomps and possessions,—that the cities, mills, farming, institutions, nations, history, are bubbles filled only and colored by the divine air which men blow into them, and that these, at their best, are poor things, which you will not prize at the same rate, when you have learned that you can create better: for day and night, the arch of the sky, and the balls that roll forevermore in space, nourishing all their kinds, are only bubbles blown by the same divine air which through men's organs made these secondary toys. (*LL* 1: 353–54)

Writing studies benefits from revisiting this vision of the university in order to mine from it lessons for how best to facilitate change. Emerson's rhetoric and its unabashed idealism are an invitation to change our most fundamental cultural institutions and to do so in the faith that diverse approaches lead to reconciliation, even if not a grand unification. Doubt whether such change could actually occur did not stop Emerson from a persistent and pervasive belief that the yearning toward it was noble. We would benefit from embracing that belief even if accompanied by a clear-eyed view of its limitations.

Of course, an expansive rhetorical "panharmony project," or anything of its kind, will be cause for reasonable skepticism. Yet rhetoricians in particular are trained to overcome such misunderstandings and to move people to act in meaningful ways. Rhetoric aims to bridge differences through communication, and that trait, perhaps more than any other, appealed to Emerson's ongoing belief that rhetoric stood at the nexus of cultural change and individual empowerment. Emerson's legacy, then, may be to focus our discipline on a renewed purpose to reshape our cultural institutions, one that recognizes that (as he says in a rarely studied lecture that invokes the rhetorical power of Peter Ramus, Isocrates, the *Phaedrus*, and daily conversation) "every sound ends in music: The edge of every surface is tinged with prismatic rays" (*LL* 1: 151). Emerson's exhortation is to recognize the music in each individual's voice, even when others don't, and his vision, grounded on that ethical stance, turns toward a greater sense of inclusiveness across all institutions.

NOTES

WORKS CITED

INDEX

NOTES

Introduction: The Architect of Discourse

1. I use the concept of "disciplinary identities" here to invoke Steven Mailloux's examination of the schism between rhetoric and literature in his *Disciplinary Identities.* That work, like so many of his other writings, helps to break down rigid boundaries in favor of expanding our professional identities.

1. "Bend to It or Die of It": Emerson and the Democratization of Plato's "True Rhetoric"

1. John S. Harrison argues that Emerson's fascination with Neo-Platonism begins with Thomas Taylor's translations and interpretations of Plato. Taylor himself was a prominent Neo-Platonist.

2. Emerson opens chapter 4 of *Nature* with an examination of the relationship between language and the natural world, an early sign of Emerson's preoccupation with the relationship between language, power, and the individual. Robert Richardson describes *Nature* as "a modern version of Plato" (233).

3. Robert Richardson's biography *Emerson: The Mind on Fire* traces Emerson's fascination with Platonism on a number of fronts, and he identifies Emerson's multiple readings of the *Phaedrus* as part of Emerson's development.

4. Emerson was fascinated with the translators and the translations. He ruminated publicly on Taylor's austere life in his lecture "Some Good Books," apparently seeing Taylor's "severe economy" as evidence of not only devotion to his craft but to Plato's core message as well (*LL* 2: 234).

5. Harrison has suggested that Emerson read from H. G. Lindberg's 1832 translations of Cousin (20).

6. I take up this metaphor in more detail in chapter 5, where I use Emerson's image of the "panharmonicon" to describe his desire for unity through variety.

7. Warren links Emerson's concept of eloquence with a search for an Adamic language, and his treatment of Emerson's lectures is notable for its scrupulous

reconstruction of Emerson's lectures on the topic. Of special note is his detailed discussion on the manuscript folders of Emerson's lectures (45–48).

8. I run into here what most who write on Cavell run into, and that is how to discuss his work without reducing his claims (if they can be called such) or spiraling into a kind of linguistic oblivion. The point I want to attune to in Cavell is his sense that Emerson, like Plato, does not limit the methods by which we name and describe moral action within a democracy. While language may, in fact, invite into it all other expressions, it does not function as a grand narrative or an essential order. How it does function is what Cavell is at pains to describe, and his point, I think, is ultimately that Emerson, Wittgenstein, and even Plato got it right by being effectively unable and unwilling to insist on anything but its slipperiness.

9. "Plato" was published in *Representative Men*, released on January 1, 1850. The essay, as with virtually all of Emerson's essays, derives from a lecture series. Emerson had been delivering the series on "great men" in the United States and abroad since 1845, and it is worth noting that at the same time, Emerson was delivering a popular lecture on "Eloquence" as well, sometimes substituting the "Plato" lecture with the "Eloquence" lecture. See Wallace Williams's excellent historical introduction in *The Collected Works*, volume 4.

10. Jill Fritz-Piggot traces echoes of Plato's *Phaedrus* in Emerson's essay "Experience." Interestingly, they are echoes more of style than of content. Fritz-Piggot focuses in large part on the similarities between Emerson's and Plato's conceptions of discourse, finding that both thinkers value lack of systemization in their modes of expression because, while Plato favored dialectic and Emerson favored the essay, such lack of system pointed to the need to work outside prevailing modes of argument (261–62). Holzwarth similarly points to Emerson's Platonic roots in discourse (322), especially in relation to conceptions of truth and political power.

11. Emerson's engagement with civic action has only recently been recovered, and this recovery is important for rhetorical studies. The frequently discussed and debated movement of rhetoric from oral to written communication in the mid-nineteenth century provides fertile ground for understanding Emerson's project. If we embrace, for instance, C. Renée Love's summary of the changes in rhetorical culture occurring during Emerson's life, we have a new way of reading Emerson's insistence on civic participation. Love, like Michael Halloran and Gerald Graff suggest, connects the loss of oratorical instruction during the nineteenth century as a loss of rhetoric for the public sphere, and if such representations are accurate, Emerson's insistence on the civic responsibility of the rhetor should be read as an attempt to negotiate this new, shifting rhetorical scene that may be trying to move away from civic discourse.

12. I will discuss both Cmiel's work and Emerson's valorization of the common man in more detail in the next chapter.

13. Berlin lodges his argument against Roberta Ray, but rhetorical scholarship has long discussed Emerson's Platonic leanings. As early as 1943, Herbert Wilchens contends that Emerson "was fond of the word *abstractionist*" and was primarily interested in generalizing principles from "different orders of experience" (512), and William Tacey argues that Emerson paraphrases Plato (25) in his insistence that the movement toward truth be the primary goal of the orator. Roberta Ray similarly reasons that Emerson's rhetoric focuses on the orator's preoccupation with making truth attractive to an audience, a point that animates John Sloan's argument that Emerson created a theory of audience adaptation that required an audience to perceive truth in an orator's words.

14. Berlin's analysis emerges at a time when foundationalism and essentialism were being dismantled by theorists. Cavell might be seen as central to this move in Emerson studies. Cavell's highly nuanced and sophisticated readings draw from a wide array of philosophical and political thought, and just as older scholarship often found itself in the shadow of Stephen Whicher's analyses of Emerson, contemporary scholarship often finds itself in the shadow of Cavell's. I find myself aligned with scholars like G. Borden Flanagan who feel that Cavell's reading of Emerson dismisses too readily Emerson's essentialist thinking: "Contrary to Cavell, Emerson's account of the soul's quest for perfection is both explicitly metaphysical and asserts a highest good, or goal, for self-perfection" (427).

15. I recognize the possible disagreement that what Emerson discusses is not a "theory." I cover that particular argument later in this study, contending that while Emerson's theory does not resemble an Aristotelian system, it is nonetheless a theoretical statement on the nature and uses of rhetoric. As such, it more closely resembles Plato's discussion on rhetoric, which instead of tracing in a taxonomic manner any particular points of implementation of theoretical ideas on the meaning and purpose of rhetoric, instead points to possibilities, encourages intellectual engagement, and challenges the very idea that the power of language can be described through any sort of system. Indeed, it suggests that reduction to system may be a sign of sophistry, something both Plato and Emerson, using different language, feared.

16. This position is solidified by Emerson's claim later in his notes and reprinted in part in the essay that even a common and lowly man speaking in his own way will, at the right moment, "hurl a sentence worthy of attention," so that anyone listening to him will become a "boy" (*CW* 7: 64). In other words, when the common man speaks a universal truth, auditors become childlike in their reliance on him and his language. He becomes the teacher, they the students.

17. Holzwarth focuses on Emerson's unabated belief that each person has a profound contribution to make to the public sphere: "His view of intellect demands that we believe that the least among us is our equal in the capacity to live well and to think independently, and that we treat others accordingly. This is an ethical step that many devoted democrats seem unwilling to take" (321).

18. I use the expression of "opportune time" purposefully. Emerson conceives of America itself as a kind of enactment of kairos, a nation whose ideas and timing meant it had special, if not ordained, opportunity to change civilization. Democracy and its inherent freedoms were part of that vision, and rhetoric provided a means for participation in a democratic government (see Roger Thompson, "Ralph Waldo Emerson and the American *Kairos*").

19. See especially pp. 25–27 in Winterowd's *Teacher's Introduction*, where his disdain for Platonic and romantic rhetoric is at times palpable.

2. Emerson, Burke, and the Limits of Ciceronian Eloquence

1. I am aware that *eloquence* and *rhetoric* are not synonymous terms, but Emerson saw eloquence as a special kind of rhetoric, one that elevated rhetoric to a philosophical realm. Inasmuch as eloquence embodied this kind of rhetoric, Emerson conflates both. In the lecture series from which "Edmund Burke" comes, Emerson uses the terms interchangeably. Even as the concept of eloquence became more important to him, he continued throughout his career to muddle poetry, rhetoric, literary essays, and all manner of expression under it.

2. In chapter 5 of this study, I use the panharmonicon as a metaphor for Emerson's lecture style, but this notion of a zigzag that from a great distance appears straight also works well.

3. I don't want to make too much about this difference between the lectures—indeed Emerson may have been assuming that his audience needed a little reminder about Burke—but the development of the lecture suggests that the opening deserves more than passing note. It illustrates rather clearly what is at stake for Emerson when discussing the life of a "great man," which is that reducing life to a timeline fails to capture the nuance of the life itself. It echoes Thoreau's "Beanfield" chapter in *Walden*, in which Thoreau's early observations about the quotidian aspects of bean farming give way to greater metaphorical exhortations for how to live a life.

4. Emerson's defense of Burke's familial devotion contrasts with his more pointed questioning of sacred cows in "Self-Reliance":

> O father, O mother, O wife, O brother, O friend, I have lived with you after appearances hitherto. Henceforward I am the truth's. Be it known unto you that henceforward I obey no law less than the eternal law. I will have no covenants but proximities. I shall endeavor to nourish my parents, to support my family, to be the chaste husband of one wife,—but these relations I must fill after a new and unprecedented way. I appeal from your customs. I must be myself. I cannot break myself any longer for you, or you. If you can love me for what I am, we shall be the happier. If you cannot, I will still seek to deserve that you should. I will not hide my tastes or aversions. I will so trust that what is deep

> is holy, that I will do strongly before the sun and moon whatever inly rejoices me, and the heart appoints. If you are noble, I will love you; if you are not, I will not hurt you and myself by hypocritical attentions. If you are true, but not in the same truth with me, cleave to your companions; I will seek my own. I do this not selfishly, but humbly and truly. It is alike your interest and mine and all men's, however long we have dwelt in lies, to live in truth. Does this sound harsh to-day? You will soon love what is dictated by your nature as well as mine, and if we follow the truth, it will bring us out safe at last.—But so you may give these friends pain. Yes, but I cannot sell my liberty and my power, to save their sensibility. (*CW* 2: 41–42)

5. Emerson mines this passage for his lecture and essay on Michel de Montaigne.

6. Emerson's work in the 1830s contains what appear to be systems or taxonomies, none of which look like systematic reasoning at all to contemporary students. Instead, they resemble pastiches of ideas loosely grouped together in lists. The structure of his first book, *Nature*, appears in such a form, as does his famous "American Scholar" speech. In the latter, which I discuss in chapter 4, Emerson describes the "three influences" on the scholar, loosely hierarchizing them while simultaneously insisting on each one's importance. As such, each represents a necessary part of a whole as opposed to a staging upward toward an ideal.

3. Rhetoric, Hermeneutics, and Submission: Emerson's Augustine and "the Art of Subliming a Private Soul"

1. "The Preacher" was published in 1880 as a pamphlet and later in Emerson's *Complete Works*, but the actual construction and delivery of it is obscured by editorial imagination and a history of multiple deliveries to diverse audiences over a period of years. Accordingly, the published lecture combines several different forms of the same lecture as well as text appropriated from other lectures, most notably from "The Rule of Life" (1867). Regardless, the first delivery occurs just as Emerson is also delivering his second lecture on "Eloquence," and it retains many of the same concerns, including a focus on the nature of persuasion and the relationship between speaker and audience. See note 1 in *W* 10: 215–21 as well as the headnote in *LL* 2: 376–77 for a detailed history of the construction of this lecture. In addition, see Albert von Frank's recent updated chronology.

2. Emerson was invited to give a lecture on Carlyle in 1881 to the Massachusetts Historical Society, but Charvat notes he did not compose a new talk and instead read from a letter and his journals (48).

3. Charles Altieri demonstrates one reason why this rhetoric may be ignored. For Altieri,

> rhetoric cannot sponsor or even ally with theology unless, as with Augustine, it is subsumed under an allegorical hermeneutics. . . . [T]he rhetorician must treat even theological claims as elements within this human drama, suspecting that theology produces its absolute object because of the unreasonably ideal and abstract demands it makes on our concepts of understanding. (96)

Altieri draws on Burke to make his claim, and while I am inclined to agree, I would suggest that it also points to the tradition I am trying to highlight. While Altieri may read that tradition as allegorical, it nonetheless requires a different conception of ethos than the one he is suggesting. In Altieri's configuration—indeed that of most of the rhetorical tradition—the rhetor is the actor in the drama. What Augustine and Emerson propose is that the rhetor is in fact simply the dress of the actor, with the actor being the godhead lurking beneath the robes. While we might question whether such a distinction is even possible, my point is only that Augustine and Emerson make that distinction and it needs to be accounted for in the rhetorical tradition.

4. Augustine attributes his discovery of God's love to his reading of Cicero. William Mallard provides a useful discussion:

> Offhand, Cicero seems an unlikely source for the love of God. Yet the discovery was a major turning point for the future theologian. Throughout the rest of his life as a Christian leader and teacher, he never abandoned the framework of thought that came clear to him in first reading Cicero. (34)

I would add that *De doctrina* illustrates this point rather clearly. Brian Stock also provides a helpful analysis of Augustine's engagement with Cicero, focusing on Augustine's early ambivalence about reading and books. Stock sees in it evidence that Augustine's hermeneutics never reveals the complete truth and that rhetoric is only effective when preceded by prayerful interpretation (see pp. 33–42 for a discussion on Cicero and pp. 181–206 for his discourse on *De doctrina*).

5. Newfield's assessment is not intended to damn Emerson in a kind of overworn criticism of the essentialistic qualities of transcendentalism. Instead, Newfield sees Emerson as profoundly antifoundationalist, and he considers Emerson as a conflicted figure who attempts without real success to negotiate the terrains of individualism and liberalism. Indeed, for Newfield, Emerson's antifoundational stance on defining the center of the human experience suggests that Emerson conceived of the self as informed by a multitude of diverse voices. This Newfield calls Emerson's "corporate individualism" (5). Nonetheless, Emerson essentially creates a kind of corporate law or authority to which the individual must submit, and the result is an Emerson who, in Newfield's final estimation, would have to overcome his own "submissive individualism"

in order to follow his own advice to "'build, therefore, your own world'" (218). In addition, see Newfield's discussion on pp. 35–39 and 154–57.

6. Emerson would use part of this passage in his essay "Literary Ethics."

7. Alan Hodder's *Emerson's Rhetoric of Revelation* is especially useful in this regard. For Hodder, the entire point of Emerson's first publication, *Nature*, is to create revelatory experiences in the reader. Hodder draws connections between Emerson's work and the biblical book of Revelation, and he traces the rhetorical similarities between the texts to illustrate how Emerson's text served as a kind of proxy for Revelation. Hodder's analysis primarily uses reader-response theory, and its invocation of *rhetoric* is in the most general sense of the term, not in the sense that I use it in this study—as a distinct intellectual tradition with its own vocabulary and philosophical preferences.

8. I deliberately borrow this phrase from Sherman Paul's once standard reading of Emerson's worldview in *Emerson's Angle of Vision*. The angle of vision suggests multiple layers of reading a text and implies Emerson's belief in the need to adopt more than one angle of seeing the world.

4. "Habit of Heat": Emerson, Belletristic Rhetoric, and the Primacy of the Imagination

1. This is perhaps an overstatement, but it nonetheless points to one of the most common readings of Emerson's romanticism as it deals with language. The point of the following section is not to provide an exhaustive survey of Emerson's romanticism—the list of works that do so is long and deep—but instead to engage with a couple of the most important recent discussions of Emerson's romanticism by literary scholars that have, to my mind, rather clear connections to his rhetoric. For more extended discussions of Emerson's romantic heritage, see, among many others, Lee Rust Brown, *The Emerson Museum: Practical Romanticism and the Pursuit of the Whole* (Cambridge, MA: Harvard University Press, 1997); Lawrence Buell, *Literary Transcendentalism: Style and Vision in the American Renaissance* (Ithaca, NY: Cornell University Press, 1973); Leon Chai, *The Romantic Foundations of the American Renaissance* (Ithaca, NY: Cornell University Press, 1987); Julie K. Ellison, *Emerson's Romantic Style* (Princeton, NJ: Princeton University Press, 1984); Kenneth Marc Harris, "Coleridge, Carlyle, and Emerson," *Essays in Literature* Fall 1989: 263–79; Patrick J. Keane, *Emerson, Romanticism, and Intuitive Reason: The Transatlantic "Light of All Our Day"* (Columbia: University of Missouri Press, 2005); Jeffrey Steele, *The Representation of the Self in the American Renaissance* (Chapel Hill: University of North Carolina Press, 1987); R. A. Yoder, *Emerson and the Orphic Poet in America* (Berkeley: University of California Press, 1978).

2. For a further discussion of rhetoric and the common man, see chapter 2 of this study. For more of my thoughts on Emerson's reading of nature as divine Word, see chapter 3.

3. For useful histories of these developments, see James A. Berlin, *Writing Instruction in Nineteenth-Century American Colleges* (Carbondale: Southern Illinois University Press, 1984); John C. Brereton, ed., *The Origins of Composition Studies in the American College, 1875–1920: A Documentary History* (Pittsburgh, PA: University of Pittsburgh Press, 1995); Jean Ferguson Carr, Stephen L. Carr, and Lucille M. Schultz, *Archives of Instruction: Nineteenth-Century Rhetorics, Readers, and Composition Books in the United States* (Carbondale: Southern Illinois University Press, 2005); Robert J. Connors, *Composition-Rhetoric: Backgrounds, Theory, and Pedagogy* (Pittsburgh, PA: University of Pittsburgh Press, 1997), 8–11. (The pages from Connors's book offer a useful survey of the scholarship on the culture immediately preceding this time.) Also see Gerald Graff, *Professing Literature: An Institutional History* (Chicago: University of Chicago Press, 1987), 17–50; Thomas Miller, *The Evolution of College English: Literacy Studies from the Puritans to the Postmoderns* (Pittsburgh, PA: University of Pittsburgh Press, 2011), 56–86.

4. Throughout this chapter, Emerson's fascination with common or vulgar speech will again be apparent. For more on this fascination, see chapter 2.

5. Indeed, scholars with rhetorical training will also recognize these immediately.

6. A version of this argument appears earlier in his journals (*JMN* 4: 10).

5. Emerson's Panharmonicon and the Sounds of a New Lecture

1. I recognize, of course, that the "rhetorical tradition" is no more set than the literary canon. My point is only that rhetorical history has been largely ignored—to a startling degree—and that some traditions in rhetoric provide obvious touchstones for Emerson's view of oratory.

2. I invoke the term "disciplinary identities" to draw attention to the history of English studies as imagined by Steven Mailloux. Mailloux, a historian of rhetoric, deftly moves between literary, philosophical, and rhetorical history to argue for greater unification of humanistic study. Mailloux is keenly aware of the intellectual divide between literary, cultural, and rhetorical theorists, and his book (published by the Modern Language Association of America) is an attempt to break down the divide by drawing on the language of literary and cultural critics to demonstrate how some key figures in those intellectual traditions, most notably Hans-Georg Gadamer, might be understood as rhetorical theorists. This study owes some of its motivation to Mailloux's project.

3. See especially Jamison's *An Unquiet Mind*, though she also addresses Emerson in *Night Falls Fast* and *Touched with Fire*. Fuller's *Emerson's Ghosts: Literature, Politics, and the Making of Americanists* suggests in a rather fine-tuned way that prominent literary critics' own sense of disappointment with culture and their own output inevitably led them to consult Emerson.

4. Emerson's frustration with literary modes is usefully seen as frustration with belletristic rhetoric, as I have tried to detail in chapter 4.

5. Genre theory would undoubtedly be helpful in framing this discussion as well. I think here especially of Amy Devitt's *Writing Genres*, which attempts to place genres within cultural contexts and argues that genres are usefully understood as rhetorical constructions intended to shape audiences. Nonetheless, genre theory, including Devitt's work, has focused overwhelmingly on written discourse, and my project here is to try to recover how Emerson's mode of lecturing attempted to disrupt a certain mode of oral delivery. Accordingly, I focus on theories of rhetoric, especially belletristic theories, that address how lecturing was theorized and how, even with its overlap with written expression, Emerson's rhetoric was disrupting audience expectations that were grounded in belletristic assumptions about public speaking.

6. Tom Wright has suggested that Emerson's lecture style was, at least in part, a response to newspapers reprinting too much of his lectures (645), and thus effectively making audiences less likely to actually pay to see him speak. If they could read what he said, the reasoning goes, why would they show up? However, while Emerson's letters and journals demonstrate his aggravation with newspapers over this matter (Bosco and Myerson have documented this well in their *Selected Lectures*, xxiv–xxv), and while he certainly was annoyed by the idea that some who had already paid to come see him might find no reason to show up once they had read paraphrases of his work, the evidence is actually quite slim that this would account for Emerson's style. Indeed, what I've tried to illustrate about his rhetoric, and what others have discussed in terms of his essays and poetry, is that he was rather self-consciously fixated, for philosophical reasons, on trying to do something new and something different in the lectern. The evidence for this latter impulse to create a new form of lecture overwhelms the gaps that would be necessary to fill between Emerson's complaints about newspaper coverage and the supposition that he would craft an entire lecture series with the purpose of being impossibly difficult to summarize in the popular press. If such is the case, we certainly have no genius at work, but instead a curmudgeonly spendthrift.

7. T. Gregory Garvey argues convincingly that among the potential results of a violation of that propriety would be violence. Garvey finds in the lectures of both Emerson and Abraham Lincoln anxiety about mob violence and potential anarchy, and he notes that even Emerson's friends recognized that invoking a controversial figure might be enough to foster discontent: "Acceptable standards of public speech were so narrow in Emerson's Boston, [George P.] Bradford's words imply, that even mentioning [Elijah] Lovejoy's name was terrifying and obnoxious" (173). Of course, Emerson, not cowed, invoked the murdered Lovejoy in order to make him an exemplar of heroism.

8. Emerson would borrow heavily from this passage in the 1843 lecture "New England: Genius, Manners, and Customs." This lecture has an extended discussion of eloquence that has yet to be addressed by scholarship.

9. I admit to a certain degree of frustration over the frequency with which this passage is quoted to demonstrate Emerson's desire for a new *essay* style.

While I would not contest that Emerson self-consciously adopts this very set of ideas in constructing his essays (he abhorred rigid and formulaic systems of expression), I'm perplexed by the number of times scholars invoke this passage to discuss essay stylistics without the slightest acknowledgment that this passage directly concerns the lyceum, rhetoric, and oratory. It illustrates, I think, the disciplinary schism that makes rhetoric invisible to certain lines of inquiry. For examples, see Julie Ellison's *Emerson's Romantic Style*, 228–29, and Cristina Kirklighter's *Traversing the Democratic Borders of the Essay*, 11. Kirklighter borrows her observation from Robert Atwan, who finds in the passage particular evidence of a distinct Emersonian essay style.

Conclusion: Distilling Emerson's Rhetorical Theory and Prospects for Future Study

1. The metaphor here is a rather indulgent play on the natural metaphors Emerson uses in his poem "Each and All," which, among other things, suggests that the meaning of a bird can only be known when it is among the trees of the forest. The narrator only truly understands the bird when he "yielded myself to the perfect whole" of the wilderness.

2. I acknowledge I am painting with broad strokes here. Of course, certain institutions have had better success recognizing diverse modes of expression than others, even as some institutions have given it serious consideration and decided, for a variety of reasons, that their institution would most benefit from retaining more traditional standards. The extensive debates around Ebonics in the 1990s was one of the most contentious examples of this, though many discussions of nonstandard English today continue to animate many campus communities. Even discussion of nonnative speakers might be considered as one of the ways that writing teachers, sometimes daily, must make complicated choices about standards of expression that veer from traditional writing expectations. Such considerations are not outside the bounds of my point here, which is simply that we may already be embracing a radical diversity of expression far more than we imagine ourselves as doing and far more than Emerson might have imagined or desired.

WORKS CITED

Adams, John Quincy. "Excitation and Management of the Passions." Adams, *Lectures* 367–89.

———. *Lectures on Rhetoric and Oratory*. Vol. 1. New York: Russell and Russell, 1962.

———. "Objections against Eloquence Considered." Adams, *Lectures* 53–72.

Altieri, Charles. "Toward a Hermeneutics Responsive to Rhetorical Theory." *Rhetoric and Hermeneutics in Our Time: A Reader*. Ed. Walter Jost and Michael J. Hyde. New Haven, CT: Yale University Press, 1997. 90–107.

Antczak, Frederick J. *Thought and Character: The Rhetoric of Democratic Education*. Ames: Iowa State University Press, 1985.

St. Augustine. *Against the Academicians and the Teacher*. Trans. Peter King. New York: Hackett, 1995.

———. *Confessions*. Trans. R. S. Pine-Coffin. New York: Penguin, 1970.

———. *On Christian Doctrine*. Trans. D. W. Robertson Jr. New York: Macmillan, 1958.

Babcock, William S. "*Caritas* and Signification in *De doctrina Christiana* 1–3." *"De doctrina Christiana": A Classic of Western Culture*. Ed. Duane W. H. Arnold and Pamela Bright. Notre Dame, IN: University of Notre Dame Press, 1995. 145–63.

Benoit, Ray. "Emerson on Plato: The Fire's Center." *American Literature* 34.4 (Jan. 1963): 487–98.

Berlin, James A. *Writing Instruction in Nineteenth-Century American Colleges*. Carbondale: Southern Illinois University Press, 1984.

Bilwakesh, Nikhil. "Emerson's Decomposition: *Parnassus*." *Nineteenth-Century Literature* 67.4 (Mar. 2013): 520–45.

Bishop, Jonathan. *Emerson on the Soul*. Cambridge, MA: Harvard University Press, 1964.

Bizzell, Patricia. "Opportunities for Feminist Research in the History of Rhetoric." *Rhetoric Review* 11.1 (Fall 1992): 50–58.

Black, Edwin. "Plato's View of Rhetoric." *Landmark Essays on Classical Greek Rhetoric*. Ed. Edward Schiappa. Davis, CA: Hermagoras Press, 1994. 83–99.

Blair, Hugh. *Lectures on Rhetoric and Belles Lettres*. Ed. Linda Ferreira-Buckley and S. Michael Halloran. Carbondale: Southern Illinois University Press, 2005.

Bode, Carl. *The American Lyceum: Town Meeting of the Mind*. New York: Oxford University Press, 1956.

Brereton, John C., ed. *The Origins of Composition Studies in the American College, 1875–1925: A Documentary History*. Pittsburgh, PA: University of Pittsburgh Press, 1995.

Brown, Lee Rust. *The Emerson Museum: Practical Romanticism and the Pursuit of the Whole*. Cambridge, MA: Harvard University Press, 1997.

Brown, Stuart Gerry. "Emerson's Platonism." *New England Quarterly* 18.3 (Sept. 1945): 325–45.

Browne, Stephen H. *Edmund Burke and the Discourse of Virtue*. Tuscaloosa: University of Alabama Press, 1993.

Buell, Lawrence. *Literary Transcendentalism: Style and Vision in the American Renaissance*. Ithaca, NY: Cornell University Press, 1973.

Bullard, Paddy. *Edmund Burke and the Art of Rhetoric*. New York: Cambridge University Press, 2011.

Burton, Philip. *Language in the "Confessions" of Augustine*. Oxford: Oxford University Press, 2007.

Cameron, Kenneth Walter. *A Commentary on Emerson's Early Lectures (1833–1836), with an Index-Concordance*. Hartford, CT: Transcendental Books, 1961.

———. *Ralph Waldo Emerson's Reading*. Raleigh, NC: Thistle Press, 1941.

Campbell, George. *The Philosophy of Rhetoric*. Ed. Lloyd F. Bitzer. Carbondale: Southern Illinois University Press, 1963.

———. *The Philosophy of Rhetoric*. Ed. Lloyd F. Bitzer. Carbondale: Southern Illinois University Press, 1988.

Carpenter, Frederic Ives. *Emerson and Asia*. New York: Haskell House, 1968.

Carr, Jean Ferguson, Stephen L. Carr, and Lucille M. Schultz. *Archives of Instruction: Nineteenth-Century Rhetorics, Readers, and Composition Books in the United States*. Carbondale: Southern Illinois University Press, 2005.

Castelaz, Donald Richard. "Fire Under the Andes: Emerson's Philosophy of Composition." Diss. University of Wisconsin, Milwaukee, 1985.

Cavadini, John C. "The Sweetness of the Word: Salvation and Rhetoric in Augustine's *De doctrina Christiana*." *"De doctrina Christiana": A Classic of Western Culture*. Ed. Duane W. H. Arnold and Pamela Bright. Notre Dame, IN: University of Notre Dame Press, 1995. 164–81.

Cavell, Stanley. *Conditions Handsome and Unhandsome: The Constitution of Emersonian Perfectionism*. Chicago: University of Chicago Press, 1990.

———. *This New yet Unapproachable America: Lectures after Emerson after Wittgenstein*. Albuquerque, NM: Living Batch Press, 1989.

Cayton, Mary Kupiec. *Emerson's Emergence: Self and Society in the Transformation of New England, 1800–1845*. Chapel Hill: University of North Carolina Press, 1989.

———. "The Making of an American Prophet: Emerson, His Audience, and the Rise of the Culture Industry in Nineteenth-Century America." *Ralph Waldo Emerson: A Collection of Critical Essays*. Ed. Lawrence Buell. Englewood Cliffs, NJ: Prentice, 1993. 77–100.

Chai, Leon. *The Romantic Foundations of the American Renaissance*. Ithaca, NY: Cornell University Press, 1987.

Channing, Edward T. *Lectures Read to the Seniors in Harvard College*. Ed. Dorothy I. Anderson and Waldo W. Braden. Carbondale: Southern Illinois University Press, 1968.

Charvat, William. *Emerson's American Lecture Engagements: A Chronological List*. New York: New York Public Library, 1961.

Cicero. *De officiis*. Trans. Walter Miller. Cambridge, MA: Harvard University Press, 1913.

———. *On Oratory and Orators*. Trans. J. S. Watson. Carbondale: Southern Illinois University Press, 1970.

Clark, Gregory, and S. Michael Halloran, eds. *Oratorical Culture in Nineteenth-Century America: Transformations in the Theory and Practice of Rhetoric*. Carbondale: Southern Illinois University Press, 1993.

Clements, William M. *Oratory in Native North America*. Tucson: University of Arizona Press, 2002.

Cmiel, Kenneth. *Democratic Eloquence: The Fight over Popular Speech in Nineteenth-Century America*. New York: William Morrow, 1990.

Cole, Phyllis. *Mary Moody Emerson and the Origins of Transcendentalism: A Family History*. New York: Oxford University Press, 1998.

Connors, Robert J. *Composition-Rhetoric: Backgrounds, Theory, and Pedagogy*. Pittsburgh, PA: University of Pittsburgh Press, 1997.

Crosswhite, James. *Deep Rhetoric: Philosophy, Reason, Violence, Justice, Wisdom*. Chicago: University of Chicago Press, 2013.

Da, Nan Z. "Emerson, China, and the Uses of Literature." *J19* 1.2 (Fall 2013): 285–313.

Devitt, Amy J. *Writing Genres*. Carbondale: Southern Illinois University Press, 2008.

Dolan, Neal, and Laura Jane Wey. "Emerson and China." *A Power to Translate the World: New Essays on Emerson and International Culture*. Ed. David LaRocca and Ricardo Miguel-Alfonso. Lebanon, NH: Dartmouth College Press, 2015. 236–48.

Donawerth, Jane. *Conversational Rhetoric: The Rise and Fall of a Women's Tradition, 1600–1900*. Carbondale: Southern Illinois University Press, 2012.

———. "Transforming the History of Rhetorical Theory." *Feminist Teacher* 7.1 (Fall 1992): 35–39.

Einboden, Jeffrey. *Islam and Romanticism: Muslim Currents from Goethe to Emerson*. London: Oneworld, 2014.

Ellison, Julie K. *Emerson's Romantic Style*. Princeton, NJ: Princeton University Press, 1984.

Emerson, Ralph Waldo. *The Collected Works of Ralph Waldo Emerson*. Ed. Robert E. Spiller et al. 10 vols. Cambridge, MA: Harvard University Press, 1971–2013.

———. *The Complete Works of Ralph Waldo Emerson*. With a biographical introduction and notes by Edward Waldo Emerson. Centenary ed. 12 vols. Boston: Houghton Mifflin, 1903–4.

———. *The Correspondence of Emerson and Carlyle*. Ed. Joseph Slater. New York: Columbia University Press, 1964.

———. *The Early Lectures of Ralph Waldo Emerson*. Ed. Stephen E. Whicher, Robert E. Spiller, and Wallace E. Williams. 3 vols. Cambridge, MA: Harvard University Press, 1959–72.

———. *The Journals and Miscellaneous Notebooks of Ralph Waldo Emerson*. Ed. William H. Gilman et al. 16 vols. Cambridge, MA: Harvard University Press, 1960–82.

———. *The Later Lectures of Ralph Waldo Emerson, 1843–1871*. Ed. Ronald A. Bosco and Joel Myerson. 2 vols. Athens: University of Georgia Press, 2001.

———. *The Letters of Ralph Waldo Emerson*. Ed. Ralph L. Rusk and Eleanor M. Tilton. 10 vols. New York: Columbia University Press, 1939, 1990–95.

———. *The Selected Lectures of Ralph Waldo Emerson*. Ed. Ronald A. Bosco and Joel Myerson. Athens: University of Georgia Press, 2005.

———. *The Topical Notebooks of Ralph Waldo Emerson*. Ed. Ralph H. Orth et al. 3 vols. Columbia: University of Missouri Press, 1990–94.

Engstrom, Sallee Fox. *The Infinitude of the Private Man: Emerson's Presence in Western New York, 1851–1861*. New York: Peter Lang, 1997.

Field, Peter S. "'The Transformation of Genius into Practical Power': Ralph Waldo Emerson and the Public Lecture." *Journal of the Early Republic* 21.3 (Fall 2001): 467–93.

Fiske, Daniel Willard. *The Book of the First American Chess Congress*. New York: Rudd and Carleton, 1859.

Flanagan, G. Borden. "Emerson's Democratic Platonism in *Representative Men*." *A Political Companion to Ralph Waldo Emerson*. Ed. Alan M. Levine and Daniel S. Malachuk. Lexington: University of Kentucky Press, 2011. 415–49.

Foner, Philip S., and Robert James Branham, eds. *Lift Every Voice: African American Oratory, 1787–1900*. Tuscaloosa: University of Alabama Press, 1998.

Friedman, Randy L. "Traditions of Pragmatism and the Myth of the Emersonian Democrat." *Transactions of the Charles S. Peirce Society* 43.1 (2007): 154–84.

Fritz-Piggot, Jill. "The Law of Adrastia: Emerson's 'Experience' and Plato's *Phaedrus*." *ATQ* 1.4 (1987): 261–71.

Fuller, Randall. *Emerson's Ghosts: Literature, Politics, and the Making of Americanists*. New York: Oxford University Press, 2011.

Garvey, T. Gregory. "Anarchy and Public Discourse: Emerson, Lincoln, and the 'Mobocratic Spirit' of the 1830s." *American Nineteenth Century History* 14.2 (2013): 161–82.

Getty, John A. *Elements of Rhetoric: Exhibiting a Methodical Arrangement of All the Important Ideas of the Ancient and Modern Rhetorical Writers; Designed for the Use of Colleges, Academies, and Schools*. Philadelphia: E. Littell, 1831.

Glenn, Cheryl. *Rhetoric Retold: Regendering the Tradition from Antiquity through the Renaissance*. Carbondale: Southern Illinois University Press, 1997.

Graff, Gerald. *Professing Literature: An Institutional History*. Chicago: University of Chicago Press, 1987.

Grimstad, Paul. *Experience and Experimental Writing: Literary Pragmatism from Emerson to the Jameses*. New York: Oxford University Press, 2013.

Gura, Philip F. *The Wisdom of Words: Language, Theology, and Literature in the New England Renaissance*. Middletown, CT: Wesleyan University Press, 1981.

Gustafson, Sandra M. *Eloquence Is Power: Oratory and Performance in Early America*. Chapel Hill: University of North Carolina Press, 2000.

Hale, Philip. "Programme of the Tenth Afternoon and Evening Concerts, with Historical and Descriptive Notes by Philip Hale." *Boston Symphony Orchestra*. Boston: C. A. Ellis, 1916.

Harris, Kenneth Marc. "Coleridge, Carlyle, and Emerson." *Essays in Literature* Fall 1989: 263–79.

Harrison, John S. *The Teachers of Emerson*. New York: Haskell House, 1966.

Hewett, Beth L. "Samuel P. Newman's *A Practical System of Rhetoric*: The Evolution of a Method." *Advances in the History of Rhetoric* 1.1 (1997): 55–68.

Hewitt, Martin. "Ralph Waldo Emerson, George Dawson, and the Control of the Lecture Platform in Mid-Nineteenth-Century Manchester." *Nineteenth-Century Prose* 25.2 (Fall 1998): 1–23.

Hodder, Alan D. "Asia." *Ralph Waldo Emerson in Context*. Ed. Wesley T. Mott. New York: Cambridge University Press, 2014. 40–48.

———. "'The Best of Brahmins': India Reading Emerson Reading India." *Ralph Waldo Emerson: Bicentenary Appraisals*. Ed. Barry Tharaud. Trier, Germany: Wissenschaftlicher Verlag, 2006. 177–201.

———. *Emerson's Rhetoric of Revelation: "Nature," the Reader, and the Apocalypse Within*. University Park: Pennsylvania State University Press, 1989.

Holmes, Oliver Wendell. *Ralph Waldo Emerson*. Boston: Houghton Mifflin, 1884.

Holzwarth, John. "Emerson and the Democratization of Intellect." *Polity* 43.3 (July 2011): 313–36.

Jackson, Ronald L., II, and Elaine B. Richardson, eds. *Understanding African American Rhetoric: Classical Origins to Contemporary Innovations*. New York: Routledge, 2003.

Jahanpour, Farhang. "Ralph Waldo Emerson and the Sufis: From Puritanism to Transcendentalism." *Journal of Globalization for the Common Good* Oct. 25, 2007: n. pag. May 10, 2017. http://www.payvand.com/news/07/oct/1251.html.

Jamison, Kay Redfield. *Night Falls Fast: Understanding Suicide*. New York: Vintage, 2000.

———. *Touched with Fire: Manic-Depressive Illness and the Artistic Temperament*. New York: Free Press, 1993.

———. *An Unquiet Mind: A Memoir of Moods and Madness*. New York: Vintage, 1995.

Johnson, Glen M. "Emerson's Craft of Revision: The Composition of *Essays* (1841)." *Ralph Waldo Emerson: A Collection of Critical Essays*. Ed. Lawrence Buell. Englewood Cliffs, NJ: Prentice, 1993. 171–89.

Johnson, Nan. *Gender and Rhetorical Space in American Life, 1866–1910*. Carbondale: Southern Illinois University Press, 2002.

———. *Nineteenth-Century Rhetoric in North America*. Carbondale: Southern Illinois University Press, 1991.

Kateb, George. *Emerson and Self-Reliance*. New York: Rowman and Littlefield, 2002.

Keane, Patrick J. *Emerson, Romanticism, and Intuitive Reason: The Transatlantic "Light of All Our Day."* Columbia: University of Missouri Press, 2005.

Kirklighter, Cristina. *Traversing the Democratic Borders of the Essay*. Albany: State University of New York Press, 2002.

Kolodny, Annette. "Inventing a Feminist Discourse: Rhetoric and Resistance in Margaret Fuller's *Woman in the Nineteenth Century*." *Reclaiming Rhetorica: Women in the Rhetorical Tradition*. Ed. Andrea A. Lunsford. Pittsburgh, PA: University of Pittsburgh Press, 1995. 137–66.

LaRocca, David, and Ricardo Miguel-Alfonso, eds. *A Power to Translate the World: New Essays on Emerson and International Culture*. Lebanon, NH: Dartmouth College Press, 2015.

LaRosa, Ralph C. "Bacon and the 'Organic Method' of Emerson's Early Lectures." *English Language Notes* 8 (Dec. 1970): 107–14.

Lee, Roland F. "Emerson through Kierkegaard: Toward a Definition of Emerson's Theory of Communication." *ELH* 24.3 (Sept. 1957): 229–48.

Liebman, Sheldon W. "The Development of Emerson's Theory of Rhetoric, 1821–1836." *American Literature* 41.2 (May 1969): 178–206.

Locke, John. *An Essay concerning Human Understanding*. 1690.

Logan, Shirley Wilson. *Liberating Language: Sites of Rhetorical Education in Nineteenth-Century Black America*. Carbondale: Southern Illinois University Press, 2008.

Love, C. Renée. "The Relevance of Nineteenth-Century Rhetoric: The Decline and Revival of Civic Rhetoric." *South Atlantic Review* 71.4 (Fall 2006): 26–44.

Lunsford, Andrea A., ed. *Reclaiming Rhetorica: Women in the Rhetorical Tradition*. Pittsburgh, PA: University of Pittsburgh Press, 1995.

Maciag, Drew. *Edmund Burke in America: The Contested Career of the Father of Modern Conservatism*. Ithaca, NY: Cornell University Press, 2013.

Maelzel, Johann, and Thomas P. Jones. "Observations upon the Automaton Chess Player, Now Exhibiting in This City, by Mr. Maelzel, and upon Various Automata and Androides." *Franklin Journal and American Mechanics' Magazine* 3 (1827): 125–32.

Mailloux, Steven. *Disciplinary Identities: Rhetorical Paths of English, Speech, and Composition*. New York: Modern Language Association of America, 2006.

———. *Reception Histories: Rhetoric, Pragmatism, and American Cultural Politics*. Ithaca, NY: Cornell University Press, 1998.

Major, William, and Bryan Sinche. "Giving Emerson the Boot." *Chronicle Review* Jan. 17, 2010: n. pag. May 10, 2017. http://chronicle.com/article/Giving-Emerson-the-Boot/63512/.

Mallard, William. *Language and Love: Introducing Augustine's Religious Thought through the "Confessions" Story*. University Park: Pennsylvania State University Press, 1994.

Martin, Terence. *The Instructed Vision: Scottish Common Sense Philosophy and the Origins of American Fiction*. Bloomington: Indiana University Press, 1961.

Matthiessen, F. O. *American Renaissance: Art and Expression in the Age of Emerson and Whitman*. New York: Oxford University Press, 1941.

McGee, Sharon James, and Carolyn Handa, eds. *Discord and Direction: The Postmodern Writing Program Administrator*. Logan: Utah State University Press, 2005.

Miller, Susan. *Assuming the Positions: Cultural Pedagogy and the Politics of Commonplace Writing*. Pittsburgh, PA: University of Pittsburgh Press, 1998.

Miller, Thomas. *The Evolution of College English: Literacy Studies from the Puritans to the Postmoderns*. Pittsburgh, PA: University of Pittsburgh Press, 2011.

Mitchell, Henry H. *Black Church Beginnings: The Long-Hidden Realities of the First Years*. Grand Rapids, MI: William B. Eerdmans, 2004.

Mott, Wesley T. *"The Strains of Eloquence": Emerson and His Sermons*. University Park: Pennsylvania State University Press, 1989.

Mountford, Roxanne. *The Gendered Pulpit: Preaching in American Protestant Spaces*. Carbondale: Southern Illinois University Press, 2003.

Murphy, James J. "Saint Augustine and the Debate about a Christian Rhetoric." *Quarterly Journal of Speech* 46.4 (1960): 400–410.

Murray, James S. "Disputation, Deception, and Dialectic: Plato on the True Rhetoric (*Phaedrus* 261–266)." *Philosophy and Rhetoric* 21.4 (Fall 1988): 279–89.

Newfield, Christopher. *The Emerson Effect: Individualism and Submission in America*. Chicago: University of Chicago Press, 1996.

Newman, Samuel P. *A Practical System of Rhetoric; or the Principles and Rules of Style, Inferred from Examples of Writing; to Which Is Added a Historical Dissertation on English Style*. 12th ed. New York: M. H. Newman, 1843.

Nunley, Vorris L. "From the Harbor to Da Academic Hood: Hush Harbors and an African American Rhetorical Tradition." *African American Rhetoric(s): Interdisciplinary Perspectives*. Ed. Elaine B. Richardson and Ronald L. Jackson II. Carbondale: Southern Illinois University Press, 2004. 221–41.

Olson, Gary A. "Toward a Post-Process Composition: Abandoning the Rhetoric of Assertion." *Post-Process Theory: Beyond the Writing-Process Paradigm*. Ed. Thomas Kent. Carbondale: Southern Illinois University Press, 1999. 7–15.

Packer, B. L. *Emerson's Fall: A New Interpretation of the Major Essays*. New York: Continuum, 1982.

Partridge, Richard. "Panharmonicon." *The Oxford Companion to Music*. Ed. Alison Latham. Oxford: Oxford University Press, 2011. Sept. 1, 2015.

Paul, Sherman. *Emerson's Angle of Vision: Man and Nature in American Experience*. Cambridge, MA: Harvard University Press, 1952.

Petraglia, Joseph. "Is There Life After Process? The Role of Social Scientism in a Changing Discipline." *Post-Process Theory: Beyond the Writing-Process Paradigm*. Ed. Thomas Kent. Carbondale: Southern Illinois University Press, 1999. 49–64.

Plato. *Gorgias*. Trans. Donald J. Zeyl. Indianapolis, IN: Hackett, 1987.

———. *Phaedrus and Letters 7 and 8*. Trans. Walter Hamilton. New York: Penguin, 1973.

———. *The Works of Plato, Viz His Fifty-Five Dialogues, and Twelve Epistles*. Trans. Thomas Taylor and Floyer Sydenham. 5 vols. London: R. Wilks, 1804.

Poirier, Richard. *Poetry and Pragmatism*. Cambridge, MA: Harvard University Press, 1992.

Quimby, Rollin W. "The Growth of Plato's Perception of Rhetoric." *Philosophy and Rhetoric* 7.2 (Spring 1974): 71–79.

Ray, Angela. *The Lyceum and Public Culture in the Nineteenth-Century United States*. East Lansing: Michigan State University Press, 2005.

Ray, Roberta K. "The Role of the Orator in the Philosophy of Ralph Waldo Emerson." *Speech Monographs* 41.3 (1974): 215–25.

Raz, Carmel. "'The Expressive Organ within Us': Ether, Ethereality, and Early Romantic Ideas about Music and the Nerves." *Nineteenth-Century Music* 38.2 (Fall 2014): 115–44.

Reid, Christopher. "Burke as Rhetorician and Orator." *The Cambridge Companion to Edmund Burke*. Ed. David Dwan and Christopher J. Insole. New York: Cambridge University Press, 2012. 41–52.

Richardson, Elaine B., and Ronald L. Jackson II, eds. *African American Rhetoric(s): Interdisciplinary Perspectives*. Carbondale: Southern Illinois University Press, 2004.

Richardson, Robert D., Jr. *Emerson: The Mind on Fire*. Berkeley: University of California Press, 1995.

Robinson, David. *Apostle of Culture: Emerson as Preacher and Lecturer*. Philadelphia: University of Pennsylvania Press, 1982.

Roskelly, Hephzibah, and Kate Ronald. *Reason to Believe: Romanticism, Pragmatism, and the Teaching of Writing*. Albany: State University of New York Press, 1998.

Royster, Jacqueline Jones, and Gesa E. Kirsch. *Feminist Rhetorical Practices: New Horizons for Rhetoric, Composition, and Literacy Studies*. Carbondale: Southern Illinois University Press, 2012.

Rusk, Ralph L. *The Life of Ralph Waldo Emerson*. New York: Charles Scribner's Sons, 1949.

Russell, Phillips. *Emerson: The Wisest American*. New York: Brentano's, 1929.

Schildgen, Brenda Deen. "Augustine's Answer to Jacques Derrida in the *De doctrina Christiana*." *New Literary History* 25.2 (Spring 1994): 383–97.

Simmons, Nancy Craig. "Emerson and His Audiences: The New England Lectures, 1843–1844." *Emerson Bicentennial Essays*. Ed. Ronald A. Bosco and Joel Myerson. Boston: Massachusetts Historical Society, 2006. 51–85.

Sloan, John H. "'The Miraculous Uplifting': Emerson's Relationship with His Audience." *Quarterly Journal of Speech* 52.1 (1966): 10–15.

Spiller, Robert E. "From Lecture into Essay: Emerson's Method of Composition." *Literary Criterion* 5.3 (1962): 28–38.

Steele, Jeffrey. *The Representation of the Self in the American Renaissance*. Chapel Hill: University of North Carolina Press, 1987.

Stewart, Dugald. *Elements of the Philosophy of the Human Mind*. Brattleboro, VT: Fessenden, 1808.

———. *The Works of Dugald Stewart*. Vol. 4. *Philosophical Essays*. Cambridge, MA: Hilliard, 1829.

Stock, Brian. *Augustine the Reader: Meditation, Self-Knowledge, and the Ethics of Interpretation*. Cambridge: Belknap Press of Harvard University Press, 1996.

Stromberg, Ernest, ed. *American Indian Rhetorics of Survivance: Word Medicine, Word Magic*. Pittsburgh, PA: University of Pittsburgh Press, 2006.

Tacey, William S. "Emerson on Eloquence." *Today's Speech* 6.3 (1958): 23–27.

Thompson, Roger. "Ralph Waldo Emerson and the American *Kairos*." *Rhetoric and "Kairos": Essays in History, Theory, and Praxis*. Ed. Phillip Sipiora and James S. Baumlin. Albany: State University of New York Press, 2002. 187–98.

Towns, W. Stuart. *Rhetoric and Oratory in the Nineteenth-Century South: A Rhetoric of Defense*. Westport, CT: Praeger, 1998.

Uhner, Mike, and Sara Bano. "Reconciling Religion: Bulleh Shah, Ralph Waldo Emerson, and the American Transcendentalist Tradition." *Pakistaniaat* 2.1 (2010): 1–22.

von Frank, Albert J. *An Emerson Chronology*. 2nd ed. 2 vols. Albuquerque, NM: Studio Non Troppo, 2016.

von Rautenfeld, Hans. "Thinking for Thousands: Emerson's Theory of Political Representation in the Public Sphere." *American Journal of Political Science* 49.1 (Jan. 2005): 184–97.

Warren, James Perrin. *Culture of Eloquence: Oratory and Reform in Antebellum America*. University Park: Pennsylvania State University Press, 1999.

Whately, Richard. *Elements of Rhetoric*. Ed. Douglas Ehninger. Carbondale: Southern Illinois University Press, 1963.

Whicher, Stephen E. *Freedom and Fate: An Inner Life of Ralph Waldo Emerson*. Philadelphia: University of Pennsylvania Press, 1953.

Wider, Sarah Ann. *Anna Tilden: Unitarian Culture and the Problem of Self-Representation*. Athens: University of Georgia Press, 1997.

Wilchens, Herbert. "Ralph Waldo Emerson." *A History and Criticism of American Public Address*. Vol. 2. Ed. William Norwood Brigance. New York: Russell, 1943. 501–25.

Wiley, Mark. "Reading and Writing in an American Grain." *Rhetoric Review* 11.1 (Fall 1992): 133–46.

Williams, John B. *White Fire: The Influence of Emerson on Melville*. Long Beach: California State University, Long Beach Press, 1991.

Wilson, R. Jackson. *Figures of Speech: American Writers and the Literary Marketplace, from Benjamin Franklin to Emily Dickinson*. Baltimore, MD: Johns Hopkins University Press, 1990.

Winterowd, W. Ross. "Emerson and the Death of *Pathos*." *JAC* 16.1 (1996): 27–40.

Winterowd, W. Ross, and Jack Blum. *A Teacher's Introduction to Composition in the Rhetorical Tradition*. Urbana, IL: National Council of Teachers of English, 1994.

Wright, Tom F. "Listening to Emerson's 'England' at Clinton Hall, 22 January 1850." *Journal of American Studies* 46.3 (Aug. 2012): 641–62.

Yoder, R. A. *Emerson and the Orphic Poet in America*. Berkeley: University of California Press, 1978.

Zwarg, Christina. *Feminist Conversations: Fuller, Emerson, and the Play of Reading*. Ithaca, NY: Cornell University Press, 1995.

INDEX

Roger Thompson is an associate professor in the Program in Writing and Rhetoric at Stony Brook University. He previously taught at the Virginia Military Institute.